T0391257

Relationship between R&D and Financial Performance in Indian Pharmaceutical Industry

Mithun Nandy

Relationship between R&D and Financial Performance in Indian Pharmaceutical Industry

palgrave
macmillan

Mithun Nandy
Hegde & Hegde Pharmaceutica LLP
Mumbai, Maharashtra, India

ISBN 978-981-16-6920-0   ISBN 978-981-16-6921-7   (eBook)
https://doi.org/10.1007/978-981-16-6921-7

This Palgrave Macmillan imprint is published by the registered company Springer Nature
Singapore Pte Ltd.
The registered company address is: 152 Beach Road, #21-01/04 Gateway East, Singapore
189721, Singapore

Dedicated to my respected Maa (Mother) Smt.Ila Nandy and Baba (Father) Shri Swapan Kumar Nandy who have sacrificed their whole life in my upbringing and provided me enormous freedom to chase my colourful dreams both in my corporate career as well as in my academic aspirations for producing quality research works and creating an impact in the world.

PREFACE

It's imperative to mention that in emerging economies like India providing right medicine at the right time and at the right place with an affordable price is really a challenging task for the Indian pharmaceutical companies. However, these challenges are being managed by the Indian pharmaceutical companies by being proactive and not being reactive and hence Indian pharmaceutical companies have been constantly taking an endeavour for providing innovative and satisfactory healthcare solutions to the needy patients by conducting different research and development (R&D) activities. Earlier Indian pharmaceutical companies used to solely depend on multinational pharmaceutical companies (MNCs) for importing quality drugs towards serving needy patients. But in the last three decades the scenario has been changed. After studying the literature review it has been found that at present there is a wide gap of information in the area of research and development (R&D) activities of Indian pharmaceutical companies and its subsequent impact on the financial performance. Though there are some studies available in the research and development (R&D) area pertains to the pharmaceutical industry, but almost all of them have been conducted in the context of United States of America (USA) and other foreign countries. A few Indian researchers have made commendable efforts to bridge the gap, but owing to the lack of serious efforts, the impact of research and development (R&D) activities of Indian pharmaceutical companies on their financial performance is unexplored and for this reason an attempt has been taken to conduct the study and get this documented in a book format.

The special features of this book are briefly outlined below.

I. The book has been designed based on the empirical study and each chapter in the book starts with an introductory paragraph that states the objectives of the study and the means adopted to achieve them.

II. This book maintains simple and effective language, cogent presentation, and clarity of exposition, self-contained and practical approach so as to make the expression clear and lucid.

III. The originality of this book like: concepts, techniques and applications have been related to the Indian context but having implications in global context.

IV. The orientation of the book is towards applied approach. To have a better and thoughtful understanding of the study which has been documented in the book, following four (4) objectives have been set.

(1) To study the nature and extent of marketing activities of Indian pharmaceutical companies.

(2) To study the research and development activities of different Indian pharmaceutical companies.

(3) To look into the Global Competitiveness of Indian Pharmaceutical Industry—Trends and Strategies.

(4) To study the relationship between research and development activities and financial performance of Indian pharmaceutical companies.

So, when the reader will go through the book, it will be highly comfortable for the reader to connect all the facts and figures stated in the book in a chronological manner.

To satisfy the above-mentioned objectives, the relevant discussion has been made in a comprehensive manner and relates its facts and contents in the light of the Indian context.

V. This book features a balanced combination of descriptive and empirical research work. It is divided into seven (7) parts. One of which is devoted entirely to the Empirical Study. The other six (6) parts systematically cover the other different aspects of the book.

VI. Contemporary statistical tools and techniques (Panel Data Analysis) have been incorporated for empirical analysis purpose.

VII. The reading matter in each chapter is divided into sections and subsections which are logically connected to each other. There is a very small amount of deliberate repetition to enable reinforcement of reading matter and to make reader for comfortable.

VIII. The structure of the textual matter written in the different chapters is on the basis of certain ideas that have been imbibed for the writings of several pioneers in this field. The complete chapter plan of the book is shown in the following.

Chapter 1—**Introduction to Pharmaceutical Marketing**: Specifically describes Backdrop, Evolution, Conceptual Model, and An Insight pertain to Indian Pharmaceutical Industry (IPI). This section also deals with the Literature Review, Research Gap, Objectives of the Study, Hypotheses, Research Methodology and at last Plan of the Study.

Chapter 2—**A Profile of the MNC Subsidiaries & Indian Pharmaceutical Companies**: This chapter mainly focuses on the 'Profile' and 'Operational Areas' of different Indian pharmaceutical companies.

Chapter 3—**Marketing Activities of Indian Pharmaceutical Companies**: Includes different marketing activities practiced by Indian pharmaceutical companies.

Chapter 4—**Research and Development Activities of the Indian Pharmaceutical Companies**: Deals with different types of research and development (R&D) activities performed by Indian pharmaceutical companies.

Chapter 5—**Global Competitiveness of Indian Pharmaceutical Companies**: Discusses how different Indian pharmaceutical companies are attaining global competitiveness in international platform.

Chapter 6—**Evaluation of Financial Performance in the Global Context**: This chapter discusses how the financial performance has been measured by different academicians and researchers in global context.

Chapter 7—**Empirical Study**: This section mainly deals with the empirical study which establishes a link between research and development (R&D) activities and financial performance of listed Indian pharmaceutical companies. The chapter also draws the conclusion based on the discussion made in the previous chapters in a very short and simple manner.

Mumbai, India   Mithun Nandy

ACKNOWLEDGEMENTS

First of all I would like to extend my deep sense of gratitude and heartfelt thanks to my Ph.D. Supervisor Dr. Brajaballav Pal, Associate Professor, Department of Commerce, Vidyasagar University, Midnapore, India for providing his immense intellectual and motivational support during the journey of my doctoral study. I would also like to express my sincere thanks and warm regards to Dr. Debasish Biswas, Assistant Professor and Head of the Department and Dr. Tarak Nath Sahu, Assistant Professor, Department of Business Administration, Vidyasagar University for providing their motivational support and encouragement in all my academic efforts and endeavours. I would also like to extend my heartfelt thanks and warm regards to Professor Kamal K. Kar, Department of Mechanical Engineering and Materials Science Programme, Indian Institute of Technology (IIT), Kanpur for providing his continuous motivation to travel in the path of innovation and creativity. My heartfelt and sincere thanks to Professor (Dr.) P. S. Das, retired professor of Vinod Gupta School of Management (VGSOM), IIT–Kharagpur for providing his blessings and best wishes in all my academic endeavours.

From the core of my heart I would like to extend my heartfelt thanks and convey warm regards to Dr. Sudhir Rana, Faculty, College of Healthcare Management and Economics, Gulf Medical University, UAE for providing his constant motivation and encouragements for producing quality research work in the area of healthcare management as well as accomplishing this book writing project. I am also indebted to him for the arrangement of content reproduction permission in this book pertaining to my own published empirical research article in the Scoupus indexed Sage Publication journal: *FIIB Business Review (FBR)* where he is the honourable Editor-in-Chief.

I would like to express my deep appreciation to Ms. Shruti Chanda, Research Associate, Fortune Institute of International Business, New Delhi, India and Mr. Sachin Kumar Raut, Doctoral Research Scholar, Fortune Institute of International Business, New Delhi, India and University of Agder, Norway for their motivational support and encouragements during this book publishing project.

I would also like to extend my deep sense of gratitude and sincere thanks to the Cambridge University Press and Sage Publishing for providing their generous support, wholehearted cooperation and permission for reproducing the relevant published contents in this book.

I would also like to extend my deep sense of gratitude to Swami Satyashibananda (Ashu Maharajji), Hon'ble Secretary of Sree Sree Ramkrishna Ashram, Dubrajpur, Birbhum, West Bengal, India for providing his immense spiritual and emotional support during conduction of my doctoral study and quality research works.

I also would like to express my deep sense of regards and warm gratitude to late Dr. B. V. Hegde (Designated Partner-Hon'ble Chairman) and Dr. Hemanth Hegde (Designated Partner-Hon'ble Managing Director), Hegde & Hegde Pharmaceutica LLP, Mumbai for their immense support and encouragement for having excellence in the academics.

I express deep sense of gratitude to my respected mother Mrs.Ila Nandy and father Mr. Swapan Kumar Nandy who are the inspirational force for my higher studies. My wife, Mrs. Anindita Maiti Nandy, M.Sc. (Chemistry), M.B.A. (Human Resource Management) deserves a heartfelt thank from the core of my heart whose tremendous sacrifices enabled me to complete this book writing. The exceptional help and cooperation of Master Archisman Nandy, my sweet son and record holder in the India Book of Records (IBR) with the record title *Most Academic Tests Qualified* is really commendable.

I would also like to extend my sincere thanks and warm gratitude to my mother-in-law Mrs. Lakshmi Maiti and father-in-law Mr. Bankim Behari Maiti, an alumnus of Indian Institute of Technology (IIT), Kharagpur for their constant motivational support and encouragement for my higher studies and excellence. The immense support received from my sister-in-laws and brother-in-laws is also remarkable in my all personal and professional activities.

I would also like to extend my sincere thanks to the entire Hegde & Hegde Pharmaceutica LLP, Mumbai, India family members for providing their immense support and encouragement during my professional journey in Hegde & Hegde. I am highly indebted to my learned colleagues for providing the necessary stimulus, motivation and encouragement for writing this book. I am grateful to all those persons whose writing and works have helped me in preparation of this book. I am equally grateful to the senior academicians who made extremely valuable suggestions and thus contributed in enhancing the standard of the book. I thankfully acknowledge their assistance.

My warm regards and deep sense of gratitude to respected Ms. Sandeep Kaur, Hon'ble Associate Editor, Business, Economics and Political Science Publishing, Palgrave Macmillan (Springer Nature) for taking her painstaking efforts during the journey of book review process while facilitating all sorts of communication with the undersigned author as well as distinguished reviewers.

I would like to extend my sincere thanks to Mr. Naveen Dass, Hon'ble Production Editor, Palgrave Macmillan (Springer Nature) for providing his immense support during the production process of the book.

From the core of my heart I would like to extend my heartfelt thanks, warm regards and deep sense of gratitude to the distinguished and respected reviewers for providing their valuable comments, suggestions and recommendations time to time for enriching the book to a greater height.

I would also like to extend my deep sense of gratitude and warm regards to the esteemed Management of Springer Nature Singapore Pte Ltd. for providing all sorts of support while publishing this book.

I sincerely hope that the book will immensely benefit the readers. Despite the best efforts there may be some human errors. I will, however, be obliged if these errors are brought to my notice so that in the subsequent editions the errors are eliminated. Any suggestions from the readers for the improvement of the book will be gratefully acknowledged.

Mithun Nandy

CONTENTS

ABBREVIATIONS

AIDS	Acquired immunodeficiency syndrome
ANDA	Abbreviated New Drug Application
API	Active Pharmaceutical Ingredient
ASM	Area Sales Manager
ASSOCHAM	Associated Chamber of Commerce & Industry of India
AT	Asset Turnover
BCPL	Bengal Chemicals & Pharmaceuticals Ltd.
BOP	Bottom of the Pyramid
BRICS	Brazil, Russia, India, China and South Africa
BSE	Bombay Stock Exchange
CAGR	Compounded Annual Growth Rate
CDSCO	Central Drugs Standard Control Organization
CFA	Clearing & Forwarding Agent
CII	Confederation of Indian Industry
CIS	Commonwealth of Independent States
CME	Continuing Medical Education
CNS	Central Nervous System
COPD	Chronic Obstructive Pulmonary Disorder
CRAMS	Contract Research and Manufacturing Services
CRO	Contract Research Organization
CRP	Collaborative Research Projects
DCGI	Drug Controller General of India
DL	Drug License
DMFs	Drug Master Files
DPCO	Drug Price Control Order
DTC	Direct-to-Consumer

EBIT	Earnings before Interest and Taxes
EM	Equity Multiplier
EPS	Earning Per Share
FDI	Foreign Direct Investment
FEM	Fixed Effect Model
FMCG	Fast Moving Consumer Goods
GDP	Gross Domestic Product
GOI	Government of India
GPI	Global Pharmaceutical Industry
GPM	Global Pharmaceutical Market
GPS	Global Pharmaceutical Sales
GSK	Glaxo Smith Kline
GST	Goods and Service Tax
HCP	Health Care Provider
HIV	Human Immunodeficiency Virus
HTS	Harmonized Tariff Schedule
IC	Intellectual Capital
IER	Interest Expense Rate
IFPMA	International Federation of Pharmaceutical Manufacturers Association
IPI	Indian Pharmaceutical Industry
IPM	Indian Pharmaceutical Market
IPR	Intellectual Property Rights
ITC	International Trade Centre
KISS	Keep it Simple and Short
M&A	Merger & Acquisition
MNC	Multinational Corporation
MR	Medical Representative
NBE	New Biological Entity
NCEs	New Chemical Entities
NDA	New Drug Applications
NDDD	Novel Drug Discovery and Development
NDDS	New Drug Delivery Systems
NGO	Non-Government Organizations
NMEs	New Molecular Entities
NPM	Net Profit Margin
NPPA	National Pharmaceutical Pricing Authority
NSAIDs	Nonsteroidal Anti-Inflammatory Drugs
NSE	National Stock Exchange
NSM	National Sales Manager
NVA	New Value Addition
OPM	Operating Profit Margin
OTC	Over the Counter

PDA	Panel Data Analysis
PLC	Product Life Cycle
POP	Point of Purchase
PR	Personal Relations
QC	Quality Control
R&D	Research & Development
REM	Random Effect Model
ROA	Return on Assets
ROE	Return on Equity
ROI	Return on Investment
RSM	Regional Sales Manager
RTD	Research and Technological Development
SKUs	Stock Keeping Units
SPSS	Statistical Package for the Social Sciences
SWOT	Strength, Weakness, Opportunities and Threats
T&D	Training & Development
TB	Tuberculosis
TRIPs	Trade-Related Aspects of Intellectual Property Rights
TRR	Tax Retention Rate
UN	United Nations
UNICEF	United Nations International Children's Fund
USFDA	United States Food and Drug Administration
USP	Unique Selling Propositions
VAIC	Value Added Intellectual Coefficient
VIF	Variation Inflation Factor
WEF	World Economic Forum
WHO	World Health Organization
WTO	World Trade Organization
ZSM	Zonal Sales Manager

Definitions

Abbreviated New Drug Applications (ANDAs): an application submitted to the U.S. Food & Drug Administration by a generic drug manufacturer challenging a patent held by an innovator company. Once approved, an applicant may manufacture and market the generic drug product of an existing formulation to the American public.

Active Pharmaceutical Ingredient (APIs): the primary, active ingredient(s) of a final pharmaceutical product, produced in the first stage of pharmaceutical production and usually in bulk quantities.

Biological: medical preparation made from living organisms and their products, such as insulin, erythropoietin, and vaccines.

Blockbusters: industry term referring to drugs with very large sales, generally in excess of $1 billion.

Brand Name Drugs: innovator drugs patented by MNC pharmaceutical companies to prevent them from being copied or reverse engineered by other companies.

Branded Generics: generic drugs for which a drug manufacturing company has attached its brand name and may have invested in its marketing to differentiate it from other generic brands.

Bulk Drugs: the active chemical substances in powder form, the main ingredient in pharmaceuticals—chemicals having therapeutic value, used for the production of pharmaceutical formulations. Major bulk drugs include antibiotics, sulpha drugs, vitamins, steroids, and analgesics.

Drug Intermediates: these drugs are used as raw materials for the production of bulk drugs, which are either sold directly or retained by companies for the production of formulations.

Drug Master Files (DMFs): generic registration applications filed with the U.S. FDA in order to allow the active pharmaceutical ingredients (APIs) to appear in marketed drugs.

Drugs: there are two types of drugs: bulk drugs (intermediates) and formulations.

Essential Drugs: Drugs classified as essential by the Indian government consist of antibiotics, antibacterial, anti-TB, penicillin and its salts, anti-parasitic, cardiovascular drugs, erythromycin and its preparations, vitamins and pro- vitamins, vaccines (polio, human and veterinary), preparations containing insulin, caustic and other hormones, and tetracycline and its preparations. Indian companies dominate this class of drugs with a domestic Indian market share of 71 percent (%). These drugs are subject to government price controls.

Formulations: drugs ready for consumption by patients (generic drugs) sold as a brand or generic product as tablets, capsules, injectable, or syrups. Formulations can be subdivided into two categories: generic drugs and branded drugs.

Generic Drugs: copies of off-patent brand-name drugs that come in the same dosage, safety, strength, and quality and for the same intended use. These drugs are then sold under their chemical names as both over the counter and prescription forms. Also, referred to as unbranded formulations.

Hatch-Waxman Act (Drug Price Competition and Patent Restoration Act): passed in 1984, it established the ANDA process that permits the U.S. FDA to approve generic versions of approved innovator drugs without supplying clinical trials or New Drug Application (NDA) performed by the innovator company.

Innovator Drugs: are drugs with patents on their chemical formulation or on their production process. They have been tested and approved by the U.S. FDA after extensive clinical trials.

New Drug Applications (NDAs): the vehicle through which drug innovators formally propose that the U.S. FDA approve a new drug for sale and marketing in the United States.

Pharmaceuticals: are used to prevent, diagnose, treat, or cure diseases in humans and animals.

Plain Vanilla Generics: commodity generics that are 'off-patent' in the regulated markets. They offer little or no innovative value over the innovator's product.

Prescription (Rx) Drugs: medicines that encompass two classes, innovator drugs and generic drugs.

Proprietary Drugs: drugs that have a trade or brand name and are protected by a patent.

West/Western: the United States, Canada, and Western Europe.

LIST OF FIGURES

LIST OF TABLES

CHAPTER 1

Introduction to Pharmaceutical Marketing Management

1.1 OBJECTIVES, FUNCTIONS AND IMPORTANCE OF PHARMACEUTICAL MARKETING

1.1.1 Objectives

The terminology 'Market' has been obtained from a Latin word: 'marcatus' which denotes a place where business or commercial activities are taken place (Goltman, 2020; Toppr, 2021). There are two types of concepts pertaining to 'Marketing': Traditional concept and modern concept of 'marketing' which are described below:

- Traditional marketing deals with the marketing philosophies and practices which were being used in the past days.
- Whereas modern concept of marketing is very much consumer centric, it involves the design of products or services which caters to the need of the consumer fraternities and involve some commercial activities or business transactions which facilitate the transfer of ownership between the service provider (seller) and receiver (buyer) (Ishaq, 2021).

© The Author(s), under exclusive license to Springer Nature Singapore Pte Ltd. 2022
M. Nandy, *Relationship between R&D and Financial Performance in Indian Pharmaceutical Industry*,
https://doi.org/10.1007/978-981-16-6921-7_1

In broader perspectives the pharmaceutical commercial activities are connected with the direct flow of drug products from the manufacturer to the patients (Ddegjust, 2021; Ishaq, 2021; Toppr, 2021).

1.1.2   Functions of Pharmaceutical Marketing

The functions of pharmaceutical marketing are discussed in the following.

1.1.2.1   Buying

Buying is the important functions of pharmaceutical marketing management (Sambarekar, 2019). Pharmaceutical manufacturing companies procure 'active pharmaceutical ingredients' or raw materials and manufacturing equipments to manufacture its pharmaceutical or drug products. Similarly, different intermediaries or middlemen such as super-stockiest or wholesaler, distributors and retailers or chemists counters have to purchase the drug products from various sources of supply to sell it with a profit margin to consumers or patients or end users (Ecelpros, 2021; Greenlight Guru, 2021; Idunote, 2021; Sambarekar, 2019). There are four methods of buying:

- By inspection: In this method, the buyer or his authorized person or agent visit the commercial premises of the seller for inspection of the goods which is proposed to be purchased followed by rational purchasing decision (Idunote, 2021; Sambarekar, 2019).
- By sample: It is very common method of purchase of drug products. The sample of goods is supplied by the supplier for its approval from the buyer and to obtain judicious decision from the buyer whether to receive the product or reject the product (Greenlight Guru, 2021; Idunote, 2021).
- By description: It deals with the purchases of drug products made on the basis description of pharmaceutical product in the catalogue or price-list of the supplier (Ecelpros, 2021; Greenlight Guru, 2021).
- By grades: The drug or pharmaceutical product which are standardized and graded at purchasing compatible followed by all norms and compliance in required quantity simply by mentioning their grade, e.g. 'Indian Standards Institute (ISI)', 'International Pharmacopoeia (I.P.)', 'British Pharmacopoeia (B.P.)', 'United States Pharmacopeia (USP)', etc. (Ecelpros, 2021; Idunote, 2021).

1.1.2.2 Selling

Selling is the crucial part of marketing management and this is also an integral function of marketing management. Selling and buying commercial activities are interconnected with each other. Basically it is the process through which goods and services finally channelize to the end-user who needs them and the companies perform their function of distributing products and services among consumers (Businessmanagementideas, 2021).

1.1.2.3 Transportation

Transportation deals with the movement of goods. By adopting this method, people from one place to another connect places in a systematic manner. Mass production and selling is hardly possible in absence of efficient, economical and systematized transportation system.

- It helps in stabilization of prices of commodities by movement of supplies from surplus to the deficient areas.
- It helps in the promotion of several industries production perishable article.
- It is indispensable for the assembling and distribution of raw materials which helps in production of finished goods without any interruption.

1.1.2.4 Storage

It involves the making of proper arrangements for retaining goods in a perfect state till they are needed by consumers. It also involves the following activities.

- It helps to maintain stability of prices.
- It helps to make sure the availability and convenience of goods for future needs and supply purposes.
- This aspect is of great importance to us as certain essential substances required in everyday life such as drugs, chemicals and medicines required to be stored properly for preventing them from being damaged.

1.1.2.5 Grading

- It ensures goods of standard quality to the consumers.

- It enables the seller to sell by sample and description. This helps in widening the market of a particular commodity.
- It facilitates distribution of goods at every stage.
- It assists the seller to obtain a better price for a particular drug product.
- It greatly reduces the advertising cost and the cost of sales promotion.

1.1.2.6   Packing and Packaging

Packing is related to the wrapping, crating, filling and compression, etc., of goods. Whereas packaging is concerned with the creation and designing of proper packages for different products.

- It facilitates handling of the product.
- It ensures the product supply with right quality, quantity and weight to the consumer without any spoilage, breakage and leakage during transportation.
- It promotes sale as aesthetic packaging attracts the attention of consumers.
- It greatly helps in marketing and advertising of a particular drug product.
- It also does have a repack and resale value for the consumer in post-use of the product.

1.1.2.7   Financing

The marketing aspects do require both fixed and working capital. The wholesaler, retailer, commission agent, broker, cooperative undertakings and sales department of a manufacturer need a quite a huge amount of capital for the purchase of goods for resale, paying of wages and salaries. The capital involved in this aspect is related to as the working capital. On the other hand, fixed capital is essential for the purchase of land, building, machinery and furniture. Finance is needed for the following purposes:

- To maintain the minimum level of inventories in anticipation of the demand.
- To meet the buying, selling and transport expenses.
- To provide credit facility to the consumer.
- To meet changes in style, fashion and competitive products.

- To regulate the production and the storage of goods, in demand, during a particular season.

1.1.2.8 Feedback Information

Feedback information is required for proper running of business. The management collects information regarding demand, supply, latest trend of market and future demand of their items through proper market research.

- It provides immense help to launch the new products in market after conducting the proper survey about the market.
- It helps manufacturer to find out other similar or me-too products available in different markets where the manufacturing or marketing company operates in.

1.1.2.9 Importance of Pharmaceutical Marketing

How marketing of pharmaceutical products influence the consumers are discussed below.

(a) Influence of non-purchasers on the purchasing habits of the consumer.
(b) Authorization powers of physicians—prescription (Rx) made by the healthcare provider is a legitimate and an authorized document for the patient fraternities to buy medicine from the chemists counters.
(c) Classification of markets, identifying the different diseases and disorders are also being catered through the pharmaceutical marketing.
(d) Professional licensing required for stocking and selling pharmaceutical products.
(e) Records of every transaction are kept that specific to patient, physician and product.

1.2 MARKETING VS PHARMACEUTICAL MARKETING

A brief discussion about marketing and pharmaceutical marketing is described herewith. There are certain distinctions which are presented below in a tabular form (Table 1.1).

Table 1.1 Differences between marketing and pharmaceutical marketing

Sl.No	Marketing	Pharmaceutical marketing
1	'Western art of marketing and distribution' has defined marketing as 'the action or business of promoting and selling products or services, including market research and advertising'	Pharmaceutical marketing refers to the marketing of healthcare solution or drugs and medical devices. It also deals with many stakeholders like private and public hospitals doctors, clinicians and patient fraternities
2	No licence as such is needed to market fast moving consumer goods or over-the-counter products	Proper drug licence is essential to deal in pharmaceutical marketing. All drugs should be marketed with necessary legitimate licences and required regulatory approvals
3	With basic sales knowledge a person can start his marketing career	The practitioner in pharmaceutical marketing domain is a knowledge based person who has the required knowledge about drugs or molecules. The person who promotes drug to the doctors is recognized as the Medical Representative who is also accustomed with the knowledge of human anatomy and physiology. Basically the person dealing in pharmaceutical marketing must be qualified, because he has to bond with drugs, little carelessness can be harmful for the consumers or patient fraternities
4	The person in general marketing can meet every person in society for selling products and services	But in pharmaceutical marketing the sales professionals meet the focused customer group who are the doctors, clinical experts, consultants, healthcare givers or healthcare providers
5	Stringent regulation is not applicable in case marketing non-pharmaceutical products like FMCG, OTC, etc.	Pharmaceutical marketing is highly regulated

Sl.No	Marketing	Pharmaceutical marketing
6	In case general marketing there is no competent authority which governs product price or commodities	In pharmaceutical marketing there are competent authorities which closely observe the pharmaceutical products price. In India National Pharmaceutical Pricing Authority and Drug Price Control Order are very much active and vigilant in monitoring the price of pharmaceutical products being marketed by different pharmaceutical companies (Business Today, 2021)

Source Author's own

1.3   COMMENCEMENT OF PHARMACEUTICAL COMPANY CONCEPT IN INDIA

Bengal Chemicals & Pharmaceuticals Ltd. (short name: BCPL), in the past called as Bengal Chemical & Pharmaceutical Works Limited, is considered as the first Pharmaceutical Company of India. This India's first pharmaceutical company was set up on April 12, 1901, by one of the India's distinguished chemists, Acharya Prafulla Chandra Ray who is also known as 'Sir APC' (Bengal Chemicals, 2021). Initially from very humble beginning with only one factory at Maniktala (Kolkata) in the year 1905, gradually three more factories were established across India which are listed below (Bengal Chemicals, 2021).

- One at Panihati (North 24 Parganas District of West Bengal, India) in 1920 (Bengal Chemicals, 2021).
- One in Mumbai (Maharastra State, India) in 1938 (Bengal Chemicals, 2021) and
- One in Kanpur, Uttar Pradesh State, India (Bengal Chemicals, 2021).

After India's independence in the year of 15 August 1947, in 1949 the BPCL Company made its registered office at 6, Ganesh Chunder Avenue (also called G.C.Avenue), Kolkata (previously Calcutta), West Bengal State, India. Apart from this registered office of this BPCL Company also had 11 different sales outlets and 10 C&F (clearing and forwarding agencies) which were located in different parts of India (Bengal Chemicals, 2021). Initially the company started producing of quality pharmaceuticals, chemicals, drugs and household products by incorporating indigenous R&D activities, technical know-how & raw materials (Bengal Chemicals, 2021; Nandy, 2020; Pal & Nandy, 2019).

1.4   EVOLUTION OF INDIAN PHARMACEUTICAL INDUSTRY (IPI)

In the past the pharmaceutical industry of India was initially dominated by the MNCs. There were very few Indian companies doing their business operation in the India's drug and pharmaceutical market space. However, with the beginning of 'Indian Patent Act 1970', the India's central government had taken control over the country's pharmaceutical industry and covered prices of drugs. Since then, the local and home-grown pharmaceutical companies of India began to penetrate into the pharmaceutical market space and started manufacturing and marketing healthcare solution or different drug products by importing different raw materials or 'active pharmaceutical ingredients' from different countries across the globe (Govindarajan, 2016; Ukessays, 2016).

After the year 1980, further development started taking place in the pharmaceutical industry of India by putting emphasis on different parameters (Reserve Bank of India, 2021) as listed below.

- Process pertaining to development
- Production, infrastructure and
- Export initiatives.

This time period is recognized as the development phase. The growth phase took place in 1990, with expansion of domestic market place and development in the international market place in pharmaceutical sector (Reserve Bank of India, 2021). After 1990, the IPI began to invest in R&D area (Govindarajan, 2016; Nandy, 2020; Reserve Bank of India, 2021). It immensely contributed in convergence, research & innovation and new IP legislations. From 2010 onwards IPI deals with the new 'Intellectual Property Law', Discovery Research and Convergence (Govindarajan, 2016; Nandy, 2020; Reserve Bank of India, 2021).

From Fig. 1.1 we can find the evolution of IPI.

1.5   An Insight of Indian Pharmaceutical Industry (IPI) and Indian Pharmaceutical Market (IPM)

1.5.1   Indian Pharmaceutical Industry (IPI)

We need to visit the historical perspectives of IPI during the early twentieth century, when nationalism movement gave rise followed by the feeling of patriotism to a greater national interest in the areas of science and technology including pharmaceuticals.

The strong foundation to two pioneer pharmaceutical companies, which are still in existence today, marks the commencement of the modern pharmaceutical industry of India as listed below.

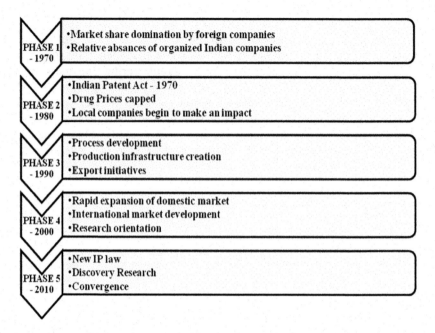

Fig. 1.1   Evolution of Indian pharmaceutical industry (*Source* Author's own)

- One is Bengal Chemical and Pharmaceutical Work (BCPW) Ltd. set up in Kolkata by eminent scientist 'Acharya Prafulla Chandra Ray' in 1905 (Bengal Chemicals, 2021; Nandy, 2020; Pal & Nandy, 2019).
- Other pharmaceutical company is Alembic Chemical Works Co. Ltd. in Vadodara, in the state of Gujrat by 'T.K Grajjar, Rajmitra and B.D. Amin' in the year 1907.

Both these pharmaceutical companies of India made a significant contribution from traditional methods of pharmaceutical production to a more scientific, research-centric and state-of-the art approach to the drug discovery, development and manufacture of pharmaceutical products (Bengal Chemicals, 2021; Nandy, 2020; Pal & Nandy, 2019). The development of IPI can be divided into three phases:

(I) IPI from 1900 to 1970
(II) IPI from 1970 to 1990

(III) IPI after 1995: Post 'Trade-Related Aspects of Intellectual Property Rights (TRIPS)' Period.

From Fig. 1.2 we can visualize the different important aspect of IPI which had been performed during the period of 1970–2010.

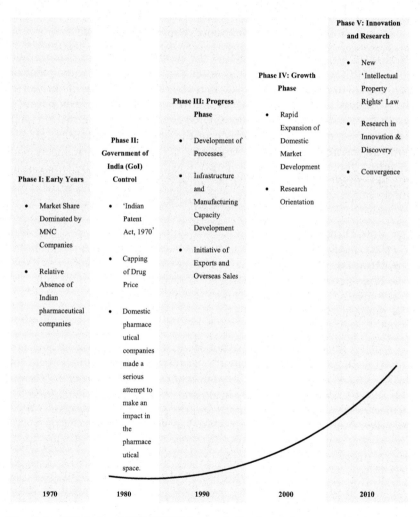

Fig. 1.2   IPI during 1970–2010 (*Source* Author's own)

1.5.2   SWOT Analysis of IPI

In the following an attempt has been made to discuss about the Strength, Weakness, Opportunities and Threats (SWOT) of IPI.

In Fig. 1.3, SWOT of IPI has been made based on relevant information available in contemporary context.

1.5.3   Indian Pharmaceutical Market (IPM)

India provides generic drugs across the globe to a greater extent. The pharmaceutical companies of India also cater to the global requirement of various generic drugs, different vaccines and other life-saving medicines to the developed nations like US, UK and other developing economies. In recent time India also is being considered as 'Pharmacy of the World' and also occupies an important position in the global pharmaceutical sector. With the meticulous effort of large number of chemical engineers and scientists, India is gradually coming up with the healthcare innovation (Nandy, 2020; Pal & Nandy, 2019). India's pharmaceutical exports are deeply connected with the following activities.

- Bulk Drugs
- Intermediates
- Drug Formulations
- Biologics and Biosimilar Drugs
- Ayush & Herbal Products and
- Surgical.

To expand the Indian pharmaceutical market, the union cabinet of Government of India has given its permission for the amendment of the existing FDI policy in the pharmaceutical sector in order to permit FDI up to 100% under the automatic route for manufacturing of medical devices and pharmaceutical and drug products subject to certain prescribed compliance and norms (Business Standard, 2021; India Brand Equity Foundation, 2021; Invest in India, 2021). With this initiative, India's drugs and pharmaceuticals sector have been attained significant FDI inflows in a cumulative manner based on the assessment made by Department of Industrial Policy and Promotion, Government of India (Business Standard, 2021; India Brand Equity Foundation, 2021; Invest in India, 2021).

Strength (S)	Weakness (W)
• Strong manufacturing base • Abundance of raw talent • No dearth of entrepreneurial scientists in India • Low cost of manpower • Low costs of manufacturing plants • Significant presence of multinational companies.	•Funding and resources issues (Low Prices & Profitability). • Lack of 'Intellectual Property Rights' (specifically 'Pre Patent Amendment Act. 2005'). • Less interest in the areas of R&D and innovation. • A weak regulatory framework & low entry barriers. • A generally weak physical infrastructure.
Threat (T)	Opportunities (O)
• Funding: Need to continuously keep-up with rapidly changing technologies. • Over-protection of domestic industry leads to isolation, retaliation & wrong signals to the Developed World. • Abroad clinical trial may provide adverse or insignificant effect on the IPI. • Lesser entrepreneurship culture may lead to significant talent loss and may act as barrier to foster drug discovery and innovation.	•Sourcing of Raw Materials, Intermediates & Bulk Drugs. • Sourcing of Generic Formulations (inclusive of United States). •Pharmacy of the world by marketing affordable medicines. • Merger & Acquisition and Joint Venture with the MNCs. • Affordable Clinical Trials. • R&D & New Drug Delivery Systems. • Early wins in New Drug Discovery. • Innovation in Biotechnology & Immunology. • Supplier of immunological for developing countries. • Bio-informatics, Biologics and biosimillar drugs.

Fig. 1.3 SWOT analysis of IPI (IPI) (*Source* Author's own)

1.5.4   Government of India (GoI) Initiatives in Indian Pharmaceutical Market (IPM)

The Government of India made a plan to set up a US$640 million venture capital fund to encourage country's drug discovery and strengthen pharmaceutical infrastructure. The 'Pharma Vision 2020' document as conceptualized by the Department of Pharmaceuticals, GoI aims to make India a major hub for end-to-end drug discovery and healthcare solution (Greatlakes, 2020; India Brand Equity Foundation, 2021). The initiatives (month and year-wise) taken by the central government of India to promote the country's pharmaceutical sector are listed below.

Month & Year	Initiatives
March 2018	The Drug Controller General of India (DCGI) announced its plans to start a single-window facility to provide consents, approvals and other information. The move is aimed at giving a push to the Make in India initiative (Livemint, 2021)
October 2018	The Government of Uttar Pradesh announced that it will take initiative for setting up six pharmaceutical parks in the state and has received investment commitments of more than INR Rs 5,000–6,000 crore (US$ 712–855 million) for the same (*Economic Times*, 2018)
Union Budget 2018–2019	The National Health Protection Scheme is largest government-funded healthcare programme in the world, which is expected to benefit 100 million poor and underprivileged families across the country by providing a medical insurance coverage of up to Rs INR 5 lacs (US$7,723.2) per family per year for secondary and tertiary care hospitalization. The programme was announced in Union Budget 2018–2019 (www.india.gov.in)

Apart from the initiatives as mentioned herein-above there are also several initiatives taken by the Government of India which are stated in the following.

- Online Pharmacies: The Government of India has formulated a plan to set up an electronic platform to regulate online pharmacies under a new policy, in order to stop any misuse of the drug being delivered through electronic supply chain where patient can avail the drug products at their door steps (Express Pharma, 2021).

• The Government of India conceptualized 'Pharma Vision 2020' document which aimed at making India a global leader in end-to-end drug manufacture and delivering world-class healthcare solution (Greatlakes, 2020).

• The Government of India introduced some innovative systems such as the 'Drug Price Control Order' and the 'National Pharmaceutical Pricing Authority' to deal with the subject matter of affordability and availability of essentials medicines (Pharmabiz, 2020).

• Under the purview of 'Make in India' initiative Government of India is constantly encouraging the budding entrepreneurs to manufacture world-class pharmaceutical products and healthcare solution indigenously and spreading the culture of entrepreneurship in R&D and innovation (Department of Biotechnology, Government of India, 2021).

India also enjoys the credit of significant number of 'Abbreviated New Drug Applications' filing and is recognized as the world's leader in 'Drug Master Files' applications with the USFDA (U.S. Food & Drug Administration, 2021). Right now Indian quality drug products are exported to more than 200 countries in the world, with the US as the key market. Generic drugs accounts for satisfactory percentage of global exports in terms of both value and volume, making the country the largest provider of generic medicines globally and expected to expand even further in coming years (Business Line, 2020; India Brand Equity Foundation, 2021).

1.6 OVERVIEW OF WORLD PHARMACEUTICAL INDUSTRY

The international pharmaceutical industry innovates, discovers, develops, produces and markets drug products for use as medications to be administered to patients to cure and ensure speedy recovery, vaccinate them, or alleviate a symptom and by treating different diseases and disorders. Multinational pharmaceutical companies deal in generic or branded drug formulations and medical devices, more specifically electronic devices. They are subject to govern different laws and regulations that govern the patenting, testing, safety, efficacy and marketing of drugs as per the applicable laws laid down in different countries (Pricewaterhousecoopers, 2010). To satisfy the worldwide healthcare need foreign pharmaceutical companies provide lots of emphasis on the following important functions:

- R&D activities
- Drug Discoveries and Innovation
- Zero Defect Manufacturing
- Faster delivery of drugs or healthcare solution
- Patient delight by treating different diseases.

Multinational pharmaceutical also takes certain endeavours patients' benefit at large.

- They deal in generic and branded medication.
- In research they try to synthesize new molecules, i.e. 'New Molecular Entities' and 'New Chemical Entities'.
- They develop in systematic and scientific approach.
- They try to sophisticated and state-of-the-art manufacturing technique.

Basically the world pharmaceutical industry is mainly responsible for the development, production and marketing of pharmaceutical products. Thus, its immense importance as a global sector is inarguable. North America is mainly considered to be the largest portion of revenue generator, due to the leading role of the US pharmaceutical industry. However, in the areas of other industries, the Chinese pharmaceutical sector has shown the highest growth rates over previous years (IMS Institute, 2020; Pricewaterhousecoopers, 2020).

1.7   Concept of 7 P's in Pharmaceutical Marketing

Once the pharmaceutical product is developed, then pharmaceutical marketers adapt the appropriate marketing strategy as well. 'Seven (7) P Formula' used globally to connect consumers for continuously evaluating and revaluating companies' financial performance. These seven Ps' are listed below:

P1	Product
P2	Price
P3	Place
P4	Promotion
P5	Packaging
P6	Positioning
P7	People

In pharmaceutical marketing the pattern or type connected to drug market, pharmaceutical products and need of patient fraternities change rapidly, nowadays pharmaceutical marketers revisit these seven Ps as expressed above in a frequent manner for ensuring their pharmaceutical business progress is on right track and try to achieve the optimum results followed by significant financial returns to gain competitive advantage over its competitors.

1.7.1   Product (P1)

The pharmaceutical marketers develop the habit of looking at the proposed product with a much concentrated approach, since pharmaceutical products only generate revenue for pharmaceutical companies. In this regard some critical questions are being asked such as:

(a) Is the proposed drug product is appropriate and suitable for the market and for which diseases it is indicated for?
(b) How the proposed/designed pharmaceutical product will be differenced from its competitors?

1.7.2   Price (P2)

The second 'P' in the formula is price. Pharmaceutical marketers develop the habit of continually examining and re-examining the prices of pharmaceutical and drug products and healthcare services and solutions being catered in market place and want to make sure that they're still appropriate and relevant to the realities in the context of current market scenario. Sometimes pharmaceutical companies need to lower the prices of its pharmaceutical products. At other times, it may be appropriate to raise the prices of innovative pharmaceutical products designed to treat different diseases and disorders owing to the involvement of substantial cost owing to R&D. Many pharmaceutical companies have found that the profitability of certain drug products or services don't justify the amount of effort and resources that put together into producing them. By raising their prices, they may lose a percentage of their customers, but the remaining percentage generates a profit on every sale (Brian Tracy International, 2021; Entrepreneur, 2004; Gandolf, 2021).

A product is only worth what customers are prepared to pay for it. The price also needs to be competitive, but this does not necessarily mean the cheapest price to offer; the small pharmaceutical companies may be able to compete with larger rivals or multinational pharmaceutical companies by providing extra value added services that will offer customer feel better to ensure value for money and customer delight. The pricing of the pharmaceutical companies must also earn a profit followed by profit centre approach to ensure the business sustainability. The 'Price Component' in the marketing mix is the only element that generates revenue, everything else represents a cost (Mcinsey & Company, 2000; Thompson, 1984).

Pharmaceutical price is being conceptualized as 'cost to the patients' which plays an important role in defining the success of any pharmaceutical marketer? Positioning of the drug product price is also equally important for the pharmaceutical marketers, the more pharmaceutical companies charge for its products, the more value or quality customers will expect for their money.

There are some pricing methods which are adopted while designing the final price of drug products by pharmaceutical marketers. A brief discussion of pricing methods is discussed below.

Price Skimming: An approach under which a producer sets a high price for a new high-end or innovative pharmaceutical product or a uniquely differentiated technical product which is the outcome of research and development and innovation.

Penetration Pricing: A marketing strategy which is used by the pharmaceutical companies to attract patient fraternities to a new pharmaceutical product or healthcare service. Penetration pricing is basically the pricing practice or strategy pertaining to offering a low price for a new pharmaceutical product or service during its initial stage offering in order to attract customers away from its rivalry or competitors operating in the same market place (Investopedia, 2021).

Psychological Pricing: This is the pricing strategy which is being designed by understanding the mindset of the consumers (Yu, 2020).

Cost-plus Pricing: Another pricing method which is used by the pharmaceutical marketers to determine the drug product is cost-plus pricing. Basically cost-plus pricing deals with a pricing strategy in which the selling price of a drug product is determined by adding a specific amount mark-up to a product's unit cost (Carlson, 2021).

1.7.3   Place (P3)

The fourth 'P' component in the pharmaceutical marketing mix is the place where the pharmaceutical product or service is actually sold out. The place basically connects the consumer with the company. The pharmaceutical marketers can sell its product portfolio in many different places. Some pharmaceutical companies use direct selling (example: through online pharmacy or electronic pharmacy) (e-pharmacy), sending their salespeople or medical representatives out to personally meet and talk with the prospective clients who are none other than the healthcare providers or doctors or clinical experts or consultants. Some sell by tele-marketing (some pharmaceutical companies hire the experts to detail about the pharmaceutical product to the doctors over telephone). Some sell through catalogues or e-mail contents. Some sell at trade shows or in retail establishments (example: during doctors conferences the pharmaceutical exhibitors keep their stall for promoting or showcase their pharmaceutical product portfolio). There are other different approaches which being adopted in selling drug products in drug market. Some of the examples are listed below.

- Some pharmaceutical companies promote and sell their pharmaceutical product portfolio through joint ventures with other similar or me-too drug products or services.
- Some pharmaceutical companies also use manufacturers' representatives or distributors to promote and sell their drug product portfolio.

• Many pharmaceutical companies use a combination of one or more of these methods as mentioned above.

In each case, the pharmaceutical marketing company must select the right choice about the most suited place for the patient fraternities to provide essential buying/decision-making information on the drug or healthcare solution which are extremely essential for the purchase decision. A brief discussion about different places which pharmaceutical companies adopt is discussed in the following.

Retail—A retailer basically is the direct connect with the end user. Concept-wise it's just opposite to the stockiest or wholesaler. Retailers or chemists in pharmaceutical trade procure drug products from the stockiest or distributor.

Wholesaler—Person or firm deal with pharmaceutical products that buys large quantity of pharmaceutical products from various producers or vendors, warehouse them and resells to retailers.

Direct Selling—Face-to-face presentation (example: during demonstration and detailing of pharmaceutical product by medical representative or MR to the healthcare providers).

1.7.4   Promotion (P4)

The 4th P of pharmaceutical marketing mix is promotion. Pharmaceutical promotion includes all the ways pharmaceutical marketers tell its customers about the drug products or services portfolio and finally ensures sells to the end users. Large, medium and small pharmaceutical companies continuously experiment with different ways of advertising, promoting and selling their drug products and services to the end users. Pharmaceutical product promotion includes activities such as:

• Branding
• Advertising
• Personal Relations
• Corporate Identity
• Sales Management
• Special Offers and Discounts
• Exhibition and Trade Shows.

Good promotion is not one-way communication; it paves the way for dialogue with customers. Pharmaceutical promotion should communicate the benefits that patient fraternities obtain from a product, and not just the feature of that product. Some promotional strategies which are being adopted by pharmaceutical marketing companies are:

Branding—An identifying symbol, words or mark that distinguishes a product or company from its competitors. Many companies spend a lot in successful brand building exercise to set up a branded medicine in the drug market space.

Example Calpol (containing paracetamol) is the brand name of Glaxo-SmithKline (GSK) Pharmaceutical Company. Calpol 500 MG Tablet is used to temporarily relieve fever and mild to moderate pain such as muscle ache, headache, toothache, arthritis, and backache.

Endorsement—A written statement addressed by a celebrity, business or professional group. The main activity of the endorser is to deliver the appropriate promotional contents for a particular pharmaceutical product being marketed by that pharmaceutical company (Singh, 2013).

Example Bollywood's distinguished actor Mr. Amitabh Bachchan collaborated with one of the India's reputed pharmaceutical company 'Mankind Pharma' as its brand ambassador/endorser to encompass the message of 'Serve life'. Through this collaboration, Mankind Pharma tried to emphasize on the importance of good health and affordable healthcare solution for the common man of India.

1.7.5   People (P5)

One of the most important P of pharmaceutical marketing mix is People or the human assets. There are wide ranges of professionals who dedicate their lives for the pharmaceutical industry. Some of the professionals who are associated with the pharmaceutical industry include:

• Drug Distribution Manager	• Professional Sales Executive
• Market Researcher & Drug Developer	• Area Sales Manager
• Pharmaceutical Purchase Manager	• Regional/Zonal Sales Manager
• Formulation Scientist	• Product Executive
• Technology Scientist	• Training & Development
• Quality Control Manager	• Human Resource Manager
• Business Development Manager	• National Sales Manager
	• R&D Expert

Most of the pharmaceutical companies spend ample amount of time to select, recruit, hire and retain the proper people, with the skills and abilities to perform the desired job. When this simple business practices are being followed, the pharmaceutical companies can successfully run the organization without much agitation and issues related to human resources. Pharmaceutical companies should also take into account for putting the right person into the right position for transmitting company's vision into ground reality.

1.7.6   Process (P6)

Process is another element of the pharmaceutical marketing mix or 7Ps. At each stage of the process, the pharmaceutical marketers try to accomplish the following:

- Deliver the value with the help of all elements connected with the marketing mix. Process, physical evidence and people also ensure enhancement of the services.
- Feedback collection in frequent manner is prerequisite for process development
- Customers are retained with the healthcare services or pharmaceutical products which are basically designed for the end users.
- The process can be designed for catering the needs of different individuals, experiencing a similar kind of service at the same time.

There are different types of processes which are discussed briefly in the following.

Technological processes: Include the process of manufacturing goods and adapting them for the needs of clients.

Example During manufacturing pharmaceutical products, the drug product has to undergo multiple processes followed by quality control checking.

Electronic Processes: There are electronic processes as well in the pharmaceutical marketing practices. After manufacturing the pharmaceutical finished product the packaging takes place followed by the barcodes on drug products which are then scanned for all official records and reference. Nowadays in pharmaceutical marketing Electronic Detailing (E-Detailing) has also been introduced as effective promotional tool.

1.7.7   Physical Evidence (P7)

In the pharmaceutical marketing mix, the physical evidence/environment is the space by which pharmaceutical companies are surrounded. To satisfy the internal customers most of the reputed pharmaceutical companies ensure the office and manufacturing units extremely environment friendly for creating the favourable working environment. The ambient conditions may include the flowing factors or a combination of the same.

- Temperature
- Colour combination
- Smell and sound
- Music and noise
- Aesthetic sense.

The ambience is mainly a package of the above-mentioned elements which consciously or subconsciously help the internal customers of the pharmaceutical company like staffs, employees and other stakeholders serving for that organization to experience the service while rendering basis job and responsibilities being entrusted to them.

1.8   Difference Between Pharmaceutical Marketing and Selling

A brief discussion between the pharmaceutical marketing and selling is presented in Table 1.2.

Table 1.2 Difference between pharmaceutical marketing and selling

Sl. No	Pharmaceutical marketing	Selling
1	In pharmaceutical marketing doctor or the healthcare provider is the primary customer for the pharmaceutical company and doctor takes the purchase decision for prescribing a drug product or pharmaceutical brand	Whereas in the selling function the end user/buyer makes the purchase decision to buy a product or service
3	In this marketing technique the demand of the drug product is being created by a medical representative through effective product promotion through detailing and prescription extraction. This technique known as 'pulling the demand'	On the contrary, in selling activities demand is created by the advertisements and point of purchase and known as 'PUSH' technique of demand creation
4	Distribution of drug products is directly controlled by the medical representatives or the field staffs	Distribution network or supply chain partners, many times act as company's sales representative at their personal capacity
5	Main source of information collection or taking feedback on market trend of the company's product portfolio is the medical representatives	In selling function company depends on the marketing consultants/research agencies for the updated and contemporary market information
6	Here, the doctor is well qualified and knows the product better than the field staffs or medical representatives	The customer/patient/end user may or may not be well qualified or aware pertaining to drug product information and the field staff knows better than the customer/patient/end user

Source Author's own

REFERENCES

Bengal Chemicals. (2021). *BCPL, the first pharmaceutical company of India.* https://bengalchemicals.co.in/

Brian Tracy International. (2021). *The seven P formula for marketing and sales success.* https://www.briantracy.com/blog/business-success/7-p-formula-marketing-and-sales-marketing-strategy-products-and-services/

Business Line. (2020). *India can become the pharmacy of the world.* https://www.thehindubusinessline.com/opinion/india-can-become-the-pharmacy-of-the-world/article31516558.ece

Business Standard. (2021). *What is Foreign Direct Investment (FDI)?* https://www.business-standard.com/about/what-is-fdi

Business Today. (2021). *National pharmaceutical pricing authority brings 81 medicines under price regulation.* https://www.businesstoday.in/latest/trends/national-pharmaceutical-pricing-authority-brings-81-medicines-under-price-regulation/story/434426.html

Businessmanagementideas. (2021). https://www.businessmanagementideas.com/marketing-management/questions-and-answers/80-marketing-questions-and-answers/18870

Carlson, R. (2021). *Defining and calculating cost-plus pricing.* https://www.thebalancesmb.com/cost-plus-pricing-393274

Ddegjust. (2021). *Basic principles of marketing and management.* http://www.ddegjust.ac.in/studymaterial/pgdapr/pgdapr-105.pdf

Department of Biotechnology. (2020). *Make in India and start-up India.* http://dbtindia.gov.in/schemes-programmes/translational-industrial-development-programmes/make-india-start-india

Ecelpros. (2021). *Standard costing in pharmaceutical manufacturing.* https://xcelpros.com/standard-costing-in-pharmaceutical-manufacturing/

Economic Times. (2018). *UP to open 6 pharma parks; gets Rs 5,000–6,000 cr commitment.* https://health.economictimes.indiatimes.com/news/pharma/up-to-open-6-pharma-parks-gets-rs-5000-6000-cr-commitment/66170849

Entrepreneur. (2004). *The 7 Ps.of marketing.* https://www.entrepreneur.com/article/70824

Express Pharma. (2021). *Online pharmacies: A rocky road ahead?* https://www.expresspharma.in/regulations-policies/online-pharmacies-a-rocky-road-ahead/

Gandolf, S. (2021). *The 7 Ps of marketing.* https://healthcaresuccess.com/blog/medical-advertising-agency/the-7-ps-of-marketing.html

Goltman, S. V. (2020). *Marketing management.* https://www.scribd.com/document/186950771/Marketing-Management-Final-Crc

Government of India. (2021). *Ayushman Bharat.* https://www.india.gov.in/spotlight/ayushman-bharat-national-health-protection-mission

Govindarajan, M. (2016). *Growth of pharmaceutical industry in India.* https://www.taxmanagementindia.com/visitor/detail_article.asp?ArticleID=6854

Greatlakes. (2020). *India's pharma vision 2020—Are we there yet?* https://www.greatlakes.edu.in/blog/indias-pharma-vision-2020-are-we-there-yet/

Greenlight Guru. (2021). *Medical device companies—Top 100 in 2020 (free chart).* https://www.greenlight.guru/blog/top-100-medical-device-companies

Idunote. (2021). *5 marketing concepts: Marketing management philosophies.* https://www.iedunote.com/marketing-concepts

Ims Institute. (2020). *Global medicines use in 2020: Outlook and implications.* https://www.iqvia.com/-/media/iqvia/pdfs/institute-reports/global-medicines-use-in-2020

India Brand Equity Foundation. (2021). *Indian pharmaceuticals industry analysis.* https://www.ibef.org/industry/indian-pharmaceuticals-industry-analysis-presentation

Invest in India. (2021). *Foreign direct investment policy of India.* https://www.investindia.gov.in/foreign-direct-investment

Investopedia. (2021). *Penetration pricing.* https://www.investopedia.com/terms/p/penetration-pricing.asp

Ishaq, S. (2021). *Marketing.* https://www.coursehero.com/file/85126740/saira-marketing-assignmentdocx/

Livemint. (2021). *Regulator plans single window system for new drug approvals.* https://www.livemint.com/Industry/76VIrrCWWE3VN9bgIMnfPN/Regulator-plans-singlewindow-system-for-new-drug-approvals.html

Mcinsey & Company. (2000). *Delivering value to customers.* https://www.mckinsey.com/business-functions/strategy-and-corporate-finance/our-insights/delivering-value-to-customers

Nandy, M. (2020). Is there any impact of R&D on financial performance? Evidence from Indian pharmaceutical companies. *FIIB Business Review, 9*(4), 319–334. https://doi.org/10.1177/2319714520981816

Pal, B., & Nandy, M. (2019). Innovation and business sustainability (IBS): Empirical evidence from Indian pharmaceutical industry (IPI). *Artificial Intelligence for Engineering Design, Analysis and Manufacturing, 33*(2), 117–128. https://doi.org/10.1017/S0890060419000040

Pharmabiz. (2020). *API units seek more sops for bulk drug sector revival.* http://pharmabiz.com/NewsDetails.aspx?aid=135783&sid=21

Pricewaterhousecoopers. (2010). Global pharma looks to India.

Pricewaterhousecoopers. (2020). Pharma 2020: Marketing the future. Prospects for growth. https://www.pwc.com/gx/en/pharma-life-sciences/pdf/global-pharma-looks-to-india-final.pdf

Reserve Bank of India. (2021). *Foreign Direct Investment flows to India.* https://www.rbi.org.in/scripts/bs_viewcontent.aspx?Id=2513

Sambarekar, S. A. (2019). *Materials management.* https://www.slideshare.net/AmrutaSambrekar/material-management-16460720

Singh, A. K. (2013). *Marketing management.* https://www.slideshare.net/networldsujeet/marketing-7-ps

Thompson, A. A. (1984). *Strategies for staying cost competitive.* https://hbr.org/1984/01/strategies-for-staying-cost-competitive

Toppr. (2021). *Business studies.* https://www.toppr.com/ask/question/the-word-markethas-come-from-the-latin-word/

U.S. Food and Drug Administration. (2021). *Drug Master Files (DMFs)*. https://www.fda.gov/drugs/forms-submission-requirements/drug-master-files-dmfs

Ukessays. (2016). *The Indian Pharmaceutical Industry*. https://www.ukessays.com/essays/economics/the-indian-pharmaceutical-industry-economics-essay.php

Which path will you take? https://www.pwc.com/gx/en/pharma-life-sciences/pdf/ph2020-marketing.pdf

Yu, E. (2020). *What is psychological pricing? 4 strategies, examples, and tactics*. https://www.priceintelligently.com/blog/bid/181764/psychological-pricing-strategy-where-s-your-head-at

CHAPTER 2

A Profile of the Indian Pharmaceutical Companies

2.1 STRUCTURE OF INDIAN PHARMACEUTICAL INDUSTRY

Before going to the detailed discussion of Indian pharmaceutical companies' profile, it's better to have a crystal clear idea pertain to the structural overview of pharmaceutical industry of Indian where different pharmaceutical companies operate and conduct manifold activities. In India, different pharmaceutical companies target a specific segment or a group of segments and accordingly design and decide their product portfolio for serving to the needy patient fraternities by serving different drug products and healthcare solution (IBEF, 2021a; Nishith Desai Associates, 2019; Mckinsey, 2020) (Fig. 2.1).

While analysing the overall structure of Indian pharma industry we can see that this specific industry is coupled with different segments or multi-structures which are shown in the following. Indian pharma industry is basically divided into the two parts which are:

- Bulk Drug and
- Formulations Segments.

Bulk drugs are mainly the active pharmaceutical ingredients with medicinal properties, which are used to manufacture formulations which different pharmaceutical companies manufacture and market the same

M. Nandy, *Relationship between R&D and Financial Performance in Indian Pharmaceutical Industry*, https://doi.org/10.1007/978-981-16-6921-7_2

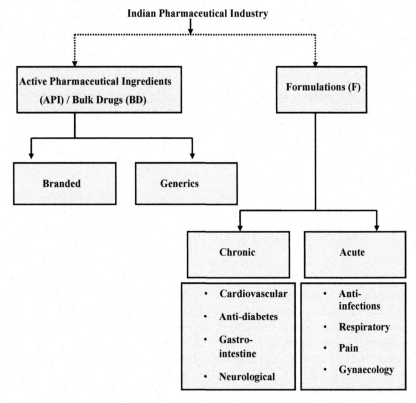

Fig. 2.1 BDF framework (BD = Bulk Drug, F = Formulations) (*Source* Author's own)

based on the mission and vision of pharmaceutical companies. A brief discussion on APIs/bulk drugs and formulations are made in the following (IBEF, 2021a; Nishith Desai Associates, 2019; Mckinsey, 2020; Pricewaterhousecoopers, 2010).

2.1.1   *Active Pharmaceutical Ingredients (API)/Bulk Drugs*

As far as active ingredient is concerned it is the ingredient in a pharmaceutical drug that is biologically active. The similar term pertaining to

API is bulk drug and the same is used in medicine. These terminologies may be applicable for natural products. Basically API is basic drug with required medicinal properties. At present, Indian Pharmaceutical Industry manufactures more than 350 (three hundred fifty) bulk drugs belonging to various therapeutic segments for treating different diseases and disorders. Bulk drug production and its exports play a major role for different Indian pharmaceutical companies (Sciencedaily, 2021; USFDA, 2015; WHO, 2011).

2.1.2   Generic Drug

USFDA has defined generic drug as: 'a generic drug is basically a medication designed in the same manner like marketed brand name drug having dosage form, strength, safety, quality, route of administration, performance characteristics which is consumed (Agarwal, 2018) by patient fraternities for recovery of different diseases and disorders'. These particular similarities help to reveal bio equivalence, which means a generic medicine provides the same clinical benefit to the needy patients as its counterpart brand name version. In other words, it can be said that a generic medicine is as an identical substitute for its brand name counterpart (Agarwal, 2018).

Basically generic drug does not hold the brand name. A generic drug must have the similar API as the original brand name formulation has (Agarwal, 2018). A generic drug which is chemically equal is having lower-cost version of a branded drug, in most of the cases the cost of generic drug is 30–80% less than the branded drug available in the market place (USFDA, 2018; Agarwal, 2018).

2.1.3   Branded Drug

Branded drug is a drug that holds a trade name or brand name and is protected by a patent (Agarwal, 2018). The patent is provided for the innovative drug product which is the outcome of R&D activities. The innovative drug that can be produced and sold only by the innovative pharmaceutical company holding the patent for innovation and drug discoveries and when the protection of patent for a branded drug gets expired, the question of generic versions of the drug comes in the picture if the USFDA agrees and provides the green signal (Agarwal, 2018). A branded drug and its generic version must hold the sameAPI,

Table 2.1   Generic vs branded drug

Generic drug name	Branded drug name	Marketing company name	Indication
Metformin	Glucophage	Bristol-Myers Squibb	First-line medication for the treatment of type 2 diabetes

Source Conceptualized by the Author

safety, dosage, usage directions, strength, quality, manufacturing date, expiry date and price in the form of maximum retail price (Agarwal, 2018). The cost of the branded drug is 30–80% more than the generic drug (Agarwal, 2018; Scientificamerican, 2004; Thakkar & Billa, 2013). Further explanation is given in the following.

From Table 2.1 we can visualize that 'Metformin', which was promoted under the brand name 'Glucophage' for the indication of type 2 diabetes, particularly in patients who are overweight. This drug is used for the treatment of 'polycystic ovary syndrome'. Limited evidence has suggested that 'Metformin' may prevent the 'cardiovascular disease & disorder', 'complications of cancer' and extremely helpful for the needy patient fraternities. It's not connected at all with weight gain. It's taken by mouth. 'Glucophage', first branded formulation of 'Metformin' produced under license by Bristol-Myers Squibb, marketed in US, from the year 1995 onwards. Generic formulations are now available after the expiry of IPR in many countries, and metformin became the widely prescribed (Rx) anti-diabetic drug of the world (Fallahzadeh, 2011).

2.1.4   Formulations

'Finished dosage' or 'formulation' is basically the shape through which the drug is taken by all of us. A dosage form of a drug is mainly composed of two things: the API, which is drug itself as well as acts as an excipient, which is the substance of the tablet, or the liquid where the API is suspended in, with other masking, stabilizing and binding agents/material that is pharmaceutically inert. Basically formulations are the end products/finished products of the manufacturing process of medicine and it can take the form of tablets, capsules, injectable or syrups, and the same can be administered directly to patients or end

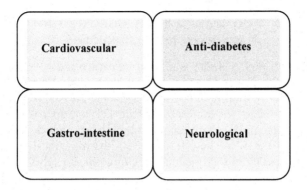

Fig. 2.2 Types of chronic diseases (*Source* Author's own)

users. Formulations can be solid, semisolid or liquid formulation. In India, formulations contribute significant influence on total Indian pharmaceutical drug exports. The growth rate pertaining to 'formulation' has managed to sustain the overall growth rate of pharmaceutical industry of India in subsequent preceding years. Formulations further classified into Chronic and Acute Diseases. In the following, short descriptions of these two types' diseases are discussed (Drug Topics, 2008; Wikipedia, 2021b).

2.1.5   Chronic Disease

U.S. National Centre for Health Statistics has defined chronic disease as 'a disease is one which lasts three months or more'. 'Chronic diseases' generally cannot be prevented by vaccines or cured by medication, nor do they just disappear. Types of chronic diseases are mentioned below (Bernell & Howard, 2016) (Fig. 2.2).

2.1.6   Acute Disease

Acute disease is considered by a relatively sudden onset of certain signs and symptoms that are usually severe (National Council on Aging, 2016). Examples of acute diseases are mentioned below.

a. Anti-infections
b. Respiratory
c. Pain
d. Gynaecology.

2.2   Company Profile of the Indian Pharmaceutical Sector

The pharma market of India is uneven in nature and is consisting with around 20,000 registered pharmaceutical companies (Nandy, 2020). IPI has stretched out radically in last three decades. There are approximately 300 large units that are noticeable in the IPI and approximately 8000 small-scale units (SSIs) are seen in this industry, which becomes the crucial part of the IPI. These leading 300 pharmaceutical companies of India which operate in the organized sector control nearly 70% of market size of India (IBEF, 2021a; Nandy, 2020; Pal & Nandy, 2019). These units manufacture pharmaceutical formulations which covers almost complete range, i.e. 'medicines ready to use' by patients and about 400 bulk drugs, i.e. chemicals with therapeutic value and used for production of pharmaceutical formulations (Nandy, 2020; Pal & Nandy, 2019). The pharmaceutical companies serving Indian pharma market clocks around 70% India's domestic demand for 'bulk drugs', 'pharmaceutical formulations', 'drug intermediates', 'chemicals', 'tablets', 'capsules', 'orals and injectable'. Indian pharma market is a tremendously unequal market proposition with different types of pharmaceutical companies as follows (Entrepreneurindia, 2020; Nandy, 2020; Ukessays, 2021).

a. Subsidiary companies of different multinational pharmaceutical companies engaging in Indian pharmaceutical space.
b. Indian pharmaceutical companies (large-size) having sales turnover greater than (>) ₹300 Crores (Nandy, 2020).

The profile of the different category-wise (as mentioned above) pharmaceutical companies engaging in pharmaceutical industry of India is discussed below.

2.3   Profile of Subsidiary Companies of Different Multinational Pharmaceutical Companies Operating in Indian Pharmaceutical Sector

During post-independence, Government of India policies for Indian pharmaceutical space encouraged multinational companies to establish pharmaceutical manufacturing bases in India. With the immense support received from the Government of India, different multinational companies came forward to set up their pharmaceutical manufacturing units in the soil of India which resulted to gain a dominant control of the IPM. Most of the subsidiary pharmaceutical companies of different MNCs' enjoyed a substantial market share: 80% till the 1970s (Department of Commerce, Government of India, 2008). The profile of some subsidiary pharmaceutical companies of MNCs which have influenced the IPM is discussed below.

2.3.1   GlaxoSmithKline Pharmaceuticals Limited (GSK India)

2.3.1.1   Company Profile

Glaxo Smith Kline Pharmaceuticals Limited (GSK India) is an Indian subsidiary of Glaxo Smith Kline Plc., a British multinational employing around 98,000 people across 150 countries. In India, this company is having its head office in Mumbai, Maharashtra, India. In 1924, the parent company started its business operation under a different name, i.e. GSK India and since then GSK India started manufacturing and selling medicines across therapeutic areas such as anti-infectives, dermatology, gynaecology, diabetes, oncology, cardiovascular diseases and respiratory diseases, as well as vaccines for critical diseases like pneumococcal disease, meningitis, hepatitis, rotavirus, whooping cough, small pox and influenza (Brandpharma, 2021; Glaxo Smith Kline, 2021).

2.3.1.2   Operational Areas

GSK India operates in the following key segments.

(a) *Pharmaceuticals*: Consisting with anti-infectives, dermatology, gynaecology, diabetes, oncology, cardiovascular diseases and respiratory diseases.

(b) *Vaccines*: Consisting with pneumococcal disease, meningitis, hepatitis, rotavirus, whooping cough, small pox and influenza.

(c) *Consumer Healthcare*: GlaxoSmithKline Consumer Healthcare Ltd., also sells nutritional and OTC products.

  a. Nutritional products like Horlicks (a 100+ year brand), Boost, Foodles, Maltova and Viva.

  b. OTC products like Crocin, Eno, Iodex and Sensodyne.

2.3.2   Sanofi India Limited

2.3.2.1   Company Profile

Since 1956, Sanofi India Limited has aligned itself with India's healthcare needs by building expertise, capability and capacity, through continued investments, strategic partnerships and a shared commitment towards patient fraternities of India. In the initial stage, Sanofi India Limited incorporated with the name: 'Hoechst Fedco Pharma Private Limited'; gradually, its name was changed to 'Hoechst Pharmaceuticals Private Limited', 'Hoechst India Limited' and 'Hoechst Marion Roussel Limited'. The shares of Sanofi India Limited traded in the BSE and the NSE (Sanofi India Limited, 2021).

2.3.2.2   Operational Areas

The company offers therapeutic solutions in the following areas.

(a) Diabetes
(b) Cardiology
(c) Consumer Health care
(d) Hospital
(e) Central Nervous System
(f) Anti-Histamines
(g) Cardiovascular Diseases
(h) Internal Medicine
(i) Oncology
(j) Vaccines and Consumer Health care
(k) Primary Health Care
(l) Arthritis and Osteoporosis.

2.3.3   Abbott India Limited

2.3.3.1   Company Profile

Abbott India Ltd. is an Indian peripheral of the American worldwide healthcare company, Abbott Laboratories. Abbott India Ltd. is having its operational head office situated in Mumbai, Maharashtra. The company has been operational since 1910 in India (Abbott India Limited, 2021).

2.3.3.2   Operational Areas

Having a healthy brand existence, Abbott India Ltd. operates in several therapeutic divisions, ranging from women's health to thyroid, diabetes, gastroenterology, pain management, neurology, urology, anti-infectives and vitamins, and Brufen, Prothiaden, Thyronorm and Leptos are the few international products of the company. Primarily four major segments the company operates and are mentioned below (Abbott India Limited, 2021):

(a) *Women's Health, Gastroenterology and Hepatic Care*: incorporating with global and local brands in the pregnancy, constipation and liver diseases segments.
(b) *General Care*: incorporating with pregnancy, pain management and vitamins.
(c) *Specialty Care*: incorporating with epilepsy, hypothyroidism, sleep disorders, depression, migraine, diabetes and vertigo.
(d) *Consumer Care:* incorporating with over-the-counter antacid segment.

The company markets a wide range of nutritional and a vitamins product for adults and patients with particular dietary needs, children and infants. Followings are the few major nutritional products:

(a) PediaSure—which is a balanced nutrition product for children.
(b) Mama's Best—which is a nutritional supplement for pregnant and breastfeeding mothers.
(c) Ensure—which is an adult nutritional product.
(d) Glucerna—which is a nutritional product for people with diabetes.
(e) Similac—which is a milk formula for infants and children.
(f) Prosure—which is a nutritional product for people with cancer and
(g) Nepro—which is a nutritional product for people with kidney diseases.

2.3.4   Astrazeneca Pharma India Limited

2.3.4.1   Company Profile

AstraZeneca India Limited (AZPIL) is subsidiary company of AstraZeneca Plc, UK, an MNC set up its organization in 1979 in India.

AstraZeneca India is having headquartered in Bengaluru, Karnataka and operates in manufacturing, sales and marketing activities of this company. The company is a listed company of NSE, India. More than 1500 dedicated employees across pan India, working for the company and delivering the life-changing medicines to patients through innovative science and global excellence in development and commercialization. The company has an advanced and innovative portfolio in critical areas of health care like oncology, respiratory, metabolic and cardiovascular diseases (Astrazeneca, 2021).

2.3.4.2   Operational Areas
The company operates in the following key segments.

(a) 'Cardiovascular', 'Renal and Metabolic diseases' (Agarwal, 2018)
(b) Oncology
(c) Respiratory
(d) Inflammation and Autoimmunity
(e) Vaccines (anti-microbial resistance, seasonal influenza).

2.3.5   Novartis India Limited

2.3.5.1   Company Profile
Novartis is Swiss Multinational Pharmaceutical Company, was started in 1996 and created across a merger between Ciba-Geigy and Sandoz. In India the Company has head office in Mumbai, Maharastra, named as Novartis India Limited. Novartis India Limited is listed with BSE and NSE of India (Agarwal, 2018; Novartis, 2021).

2.3.5.2   Operational Areas
Novartis India Limited dealing with trading and marketing of drugs and it has basically three (3) operating divisions:

Generic Medicines Division: The company runs the portfolio of biopharmaceuticals, oncology, retail generics, injectable and anti-infective.

Pharmaceuticals Division: The company has 'Gynaecology' and 'Neurosciences', 'Bone & Pain', 'Calcium Portfolio'.

Eye Care Division: The company runs its ophthalmic business through Alcon Laboratories (India) Pvt. Ltd.

2.4   Profile of Large Indian Pharmaceutical Companies Having Sales Turnover More Than (>) ₹300 Crores

With the introduction of the Indian Patents Act and the Drug Price Control Order in 1970, Indian pharmaceutical players discovered new avenues of growth, and consequently, the share of the multinationals declined. The Patent Act, 1970, opened the door to Indian pharmaceutical players by allowing reverse engineering process of known molecules under the purview of patent expiry/off patent. Owing to this, the multinationals felt discouraged to introduce their latest product portfolio (on which they had patents internationally) in the IPM. Gradually the pharmaceutical companies of India took up the manufacturing of formulations in a serious manner to provide the quality healthcare solution for taking care of healthcare need of domestic market. A brief profile of Indian large-scale pharmaceutical companies having sales turnover greater than three hundred (>300) crores is discussed below (Nandy, 2020; Pal & Nandy, 2019; Singh & Rathore, 2019).

2.4.1   *Sun Pharmaceutical Industries Limited*

2.4.1.1   *Company Profile*
Sun Pharmaceuticals, founded by Mr. Dilip Shanghvi, was established in 1983 in Vapi with five products to treat psychiatry ailments. Cardiology products were introduced in 1987 followed by gastroenterology products in 1989. Today, it is the largest chronic prescription (Rx) company in India and a market leader in 'psychiatry', 'neurology', 'cardiology', 'orthopaedics', 'ophthalmology', 'gastroenterology' and 'nephrology'. The company is listed in the BSE and NSE of India (Agarwal, 2018). Today Sun Pharma is the most profitable pharmaceutical company in India, as well as the largest pharmaceutical company in terms of market capitalization in Indian stock exchanges (Agarwal, 2018; Pharma Tips, 2012; Sun Pharmaceuticals Limited, 2021; The Business Tycoons, 2021).

2.4.1.2   *Operational Areas*
Sun pharmaceutical dedicates its business operation in the following areas and provide the quality healthcare solution.

(a) Cardiology
(b) Psychiatry
(c) Neurology
(d) Gastroenterology
(e) Diabetology
(f) Dermatology.

2.4.2   Cipla Limited

2.4.2.1   Company Profile

Initially Cipla was established in the name of 'The Chemical, Industrial & Pharmaceutical Laboratories' in the year 1935 in Mumbai, Maharastra. The founder of Cipla was Khwaja Abdul Hamied. In the later stage company's name had been changed to 'Cipla Limited' on 20 July 1984. The bulk drug manufacturing facilities of the company was approved by the USFDA (Agarwal, 2018) in the year 1985. Cipla also provided generic Acquired Immune Deficiency Syndrome and other drugs to treat needy underprivileged people in the developing world, and this was initiated by Yusuf Hamied, a Cambridge-educated chemist and son of Khwaja Abdul Hamied, Founder of Cipla. Cipla launched 'Deferiprone', the world's first ever oral iron chelator in the year 1994 (Business Standard, 2021; Cipla Limited, 2021; Wikipedia, 2021a).

In 2001, Cipla marketed HIV treatment medicines (antiretroviral) for at a fractional cost (less than $350 per year per patient). In the year 2013 Cipla acquired its own distribution partner, the South African company Cipla-Medpro (joint venture between Cipla and Medpro Pharmaceuticals), which was South Africa's third (3rd) biggest pharmaceutical company at that time period and hence the company retained it as a subsidiary with the name changed to Cipla Medpro South Africa Limited (*New York Times*, 2001; Pharma Boardroom, 2018a).

Cipla also sells active pharmaceutical ingredients to different manufacturers as well as personal care and pharmaceutical products, including Lamivudine and Fluticasone propionate and 'Escitalopram' (antidepressant medicine). These medicines are the world's largest manufacturer of antiretroviral drugs and the company is having 34 manufacturing units in 8 locations across India and also have business in 100 countries. Having a strong base over the R&D arena, Cipla's primary focus is to develop and improve on new formulations, drug delivery systems and APIs. Cipla also cooperates with other enterprises in different areas such as engineering, consulting, quality control, commissioning, project appraisal, support, and plant supply, know-how transfer (Department of Pharmacy, MVN University, 2016; Wiki2.Org, 2021).

2.4.2.2   Operational Areas
Cipla operates in the following areas/divisions:

(a) Respiratory
(b) Cardiovascular Disease
(c) Arthritis
(d) Diabetes
(e) Weight Control And Depression
(f) Skin Diseases.

2.4.3   Lupin Limited

2.4.3.1   Company Profile
Lupin was founded in 1968 by Desh Bandhu Gupta, the then Associate Professor at Birla Institute of Technology and Science, Pilani, Rajasthan, India. The company was created with a vision to fight life-threatening infectious diseases and to manufacture drugs keeping the social priority in mind. Gupta died on 26 June 2017 and was replaced as chairman by his wife, Manju Deshbandhu Gupta. Lupin first gained recognition with the world's largest manufacturers of tuberculosis drugs. The company today has a significant market share in key market segments like: cardio-vascular (prils and statins), diabetology, asthma, paediatrics, CNS, GI, anti-infectives and NSAIDs therapy segments. It also achieved a global leadership position in the anti-TB and Cephalosporin segments (*Economic Times*, 2017; Lupin Limited, 2021; Money Control, 2017; Wikipedia, 2021c).

Lupin's foray into advanced drug delivery systems has resulted in the development of platform technologies that are being used to develop value-added generic pharmaceutical. Its manufacturing facilities, spread across India and Japan, have played a critical role in enabling the company realize its global aspirations. Benchmarked to international standards, the different manufacturing facilities of Lupin are approved by the inter-national regulatory bodies including the USFDA, UK MHRA, Japan's MHLW, TGA Australia, WHO and the MCC South Africa (IBEF, 2021b; Pharma Boardroom, 2018b; Wikipedia, 2021c).

2.4.3.2   Operational Areas
(a) Anti-TB segment
(b) Cardiovascular
(c) Anti-infectives segment
(d) Oral and injectable
(e) Paediatric product.

2.4.4   Torrent Pharmaceuticals Ltd.

2.4.4.1   Company Profile

Torrent Pharmaceuticals Ltd. is the flagship pharmaceutical company of the parent group which is Torrent Group. This reputed pharmaceutical company is based in Ahmedabad, Gujarat State, India. The founder of this prestigious pharmaceutical company was Mr. U. N. Mehta. Initially the company had been formed as Trinity Laboratories Ltd., and later renamed as Torrent Pharmaceuticals Ltd. (Agarwal, 2018; Money Control, 2021; Torrent Pharma, 2021).

Torrent Pharmaceuticals is having international presence in more than 50 countries with over 1000 product registrations globally. Torrent Pharma is very much focused in the different therapeutic areas which are very much crucial nowadays such as: 'cardiovascular', 'diabetology', 'central nervous system', 'gastrointestinal', 'anti-infective' and 'pain management' segments. The company also plays an important role in the therapeutic segments like: 'oncology' and 'nephrology' as well while also strengthening its focus on 'gynaecology' and 'paediatric' segments (Agarwal, 2018; Money Control, 2021; Torrent Pharma, 2021).

2.4.4.2   Operational Areas

Torrent Pharmaceutical therapeutic portfolio has the following base.

(a) Anti-diabetic Therapy
(b) Anti-microbial Therapy
(c) Cardiovascular Therapy
(d) Dermatologic Therapy
(e) Gastrointestinal Therapy
(f) Gynaecology Therapy
(g) Nephrology
(h) Neuro-Psychiatric Therapy
(i) Oncology Therapy

(j) Pain Therapy
(k) Urology
(l) Miscellaneous.

2.4.5   *Glenmark Pharmaceuticals*

2.4.5.1   *Company Profile*

Glenmark Pharmaceuticals is the reputed pharmaceutical company in India. The company has headquarters in Mumbai, Maharastra State, India. The company was established in the year 1977 by Gracias Saldanha as a generic drug followed by API manufacturing company (Agarwal, 2018). During the initial years, the company sold its products port-folio in India, Russia and Africa. The company went to public in India during 1990s, and by being proactive taken an endeavour to build its first research facility (Agarwal, 2018). The company focuses on new drugs and biosimilars in the fields of cancer, dermatology and respiratory diseases, which it sought to monetize by partnering with multi-crore pharmaceutical companies (Agarwal, 2018; *Economic Times*, 2018; India Brand Equity Foundation, 2006; Glenmark Pharmaceuticals Limited, 2021; Nirmal Bang, 2011).

2.4.5.2   *Operational Areas*

Glenmark provides intense focus on the following areas.

- Drug discovery
- Branded formulations
- Generics formulations and
- Active APIs
- Dermatology
- Internal medicine
- Paediatrics
- Cardiovascular
- Gynaecology
- Anti-infectives
- Antibiotics
- Anti-allergic
- Anti-emetics
- ENT
- Diabetes.

REFERENCES

Abbott India Limited. (2021). *About us*. https://www.abbott.co.in/about-abb ott/abbott-india-limited.html

Agarwal, K. K. (2018). *Study on pricing policies of medicines in pharmaceutical companies*. https://www.scribd.com/document/58648418/Final-Pro-Sir

Astrazeneca. (2021). *About us*. https://www.astrazeneca.in/about-us.html

Brandpharma. (2021). *GSK India*. https://www.brandindiapharma.in/pharma ceutical-companies-india/gsk-india-ltd

Bernell, S., & Howard, S. W. (2016). *Use your words carefully: What is a chronic disease?* https://www.frontiersin.org/journals/public-health

Business Standard. (2021). *Cipla Ltd. (Cipla)—Company history*. https://www. business-standard.com/company/cipla-114/information/company-history

Cipla Limited. (2021). *Our history*. https://www.cipla.com/about-us/our-his tory

Department of Commerce, Government of India. (2008). *Strategy for increasing exports of pharmaceutical products*. https://commerce.gov.in/wp-content/ uploads/2020/02/MOC_635567633057176521_Report-Tas-Force-Pha rma-12th-Dec-08.pdf

Department of Pharmacy, MVN University. (2016). *Cipla*. https://www.fac ebook.com/974100459329104/posts/cipla-limited-is-an-indian-multinati onal-pharmaceutical-and-biotechnology-compan/1002935963112220/

Drug Topics. (2008). *Overview of pharmaceutical excipients used in tablets and capsules*. https://www.drugtopics.com/view/overview-pharmaceutical-excipi ents-used-tablets-and-capsules

Economic Times. (2017). *Lupin founder DB Gupta, a self made maverick who wanted to take out TB in India, dead*. https://economictimes.indiatimes. com/industry/healthcare/biotech/pharmaceuticals/lupin-founder-db-gupta- a-self-made-maverick-who-wanted-to-take-out-tb-in-india-dead/articleshow/ 59320216.cms?from=mdr

Economic Times. (2018). *True North in talks to buy into Glenmark's API biz for Rs 1500 cr*. https://economictimes.indiatimes.com/industry/healthcare/bio tech/pharmaceuticals/true-north-in-talks-to-buy-into-glenmarks-api-biz-for- rs-1500-cr/articleshow/65349628.cms?utm_source=contentofinterest&utm_ medium=text&utm_campaign=cppst

Entrepreneurindia. (2020). *Pharmaceutical unit*. https://www.entrepren eurindia.co/project-and-profile-details/PHARMACEUTICAL%20UNIT% 20(Automatic%20Plant%20of%20Tablet%20and%20Capsule).

Fallahzadeh, M. H. (2011). *Sample records for clomiphene citrate metformin*. https://worldwidescience.org/topicpages/c/clomiphene+citrate+metformin. html

GlaxoSmithKline. (2021). *About us*. https://india-pharma.gsk.com/en-in/abo ut-us/

Glenmark Pharmaceuticals Limited. (2021). *Evolution*. https://www.glenmarkp
harma.com/about-us/evolution

IBEF. (2021a). *Indian Pharmaceutical Industry*. https://www.ibef.org/ind
ustry/pharmaceutical-india.aspx.

IBEF. (2021b). *Lupin Limited*. https://www.ibef.org/industry/research-develo
pment-india/showcase/lupin-ltd

India Brand Equity Foundation. (2006). *Glenmark Pharmaceuticals Limited*.
https://www.ibef.org/download/glenmark_pharma_23oct.pdf.

Lupin Limited. (2021). *Dr. Desh Bandhu Gupta, Founder and Chairman of
Lupin passes away*. https://www.lupin.com/portfolio/dr-desh-bandhu-gupta-
founder-and-chairman-of-lupin-passes-away/

Mckinsey. (2020). *India Pharma 2020 propelling access and acceptance, realising
true potential*. https://www.mckinsey.com/~/media/mckinsey/dotcom/cli
ent_service/Pharma%20and%20Medical%20Products/PMP%20NEW/PDFs/
778886_India_Pharma_2020_Propelling_Access_and_Acceptance_Realising_
True_Potential.ashx

Money Control. (2017). *Desh Bandhu Gupta—The man who made Lupin
a pharma giant passes away*. https://www.moneycontrol.com/news/india/
lupin-founder-and-chairman-desh-bandhu-gupta-passes-away-2312069.html

Money Control. (2021). *Torrent Pharmaceuticals Limited*. https://www.mon
eycontrol.com/india/stockpricequote/pharmaceuticals/torrentpharmaceuti
cals/TP06

Nandy, M. (2020). Is there any impact of R&D on financial performance?
Evidence from Indian pharmaceutical companies. *FIIB Business Review, 9*(4),
319–334. https://doi.org/10.1177/2319714520981816

National Council on Aging. (2016). *Chronic vs. Acute medical conditions: What's
the difference?* https://www.ncoa.org/article/chronic-versus-acute-disease

Nirmal Bang. (2011). *Glenmark Pharmaceuticals Limited*. https://www.dsij.in/
productattachment/BrokerRecommendation/Glenmark%20Pharma.pdf

Nishith Desai Associates. (2019). *Indian Pharmaceutical Industry*. http://www.
nishithdesai.com/fileadmin/user_upload/pdfs/Research_Papers/The-Indian-
Pharmaceutical-Industry.pdf

Novartis. (2021). *Company history*. https://www.novartis.in/about-us/com
pany-history

Pal, B., & Nandy, M. (2019). Innovation and business sustainability (IBS):
Empirical evidence from Indian pharmaceutical industry (IPI). *Artificial Intelligence for Engineering Design, Analysis and Manufacturing, 33*(2), 117–128.
https://doi.org/10.1017/S0890060419000040

Pharma Boardroom. (2018a). *Cipla*. https://pharmaboardroom.com/direct
ory/cipla/

Pharma Boardroom. (2018b). *Lupin*. https://pharmaboardroom.com/direct
ory/lupin/

Pharma Tips. (2012). *Sun Pharmaceutical Industries Limited.* http://www.pha
rmatips.in/Articles/Pharma-Companies/Gujarat/Sun-Pharmaceutical-Lim
ited.aspx

Pricewaterhousecoopers. (2010). *Global pharma looks to India: Prospects for
growth.* https://www.pwc.com/gx/en/pharma-life-sciences/pdf/global-pha
rma-looks-to-india-final.pdf

Sanofi India Limited. (2021). *About us.* https://www.sanofiindialtd.com/en/
about-us

Sciencedaily. (2021). *Understanding active pharmaceutical ingredients.* https://
www.sciencedaily.com/releases/2014/06/140605093305.htm#:~:text=Act
ive%20pharmaceutical%20ingredient%20(API)%2C,(e.g.%20tablet%2C%20c
apsule).

Scientificamerican. (2004). *What's the difference between brand-name and generic
prescription drugs?* https://www.scientificamerican.com/article/whats-the-dif
ference-betw-2004-12-13/

Singh, R. S., & Rathore, V. (2019). *India: New drugs patented under the
'Indian Patent Act, 1970' are outside the price control for the first 5 years from
their commercial marketing.* https://www.mondaq.com/india/patent/782
384/new-drugs-patented-under-the-indian-patent-act-1970-are-outside-the-
price-control-for-the-first-5-years-from-their-commercial-marketing

Sun Pharmaceuticals Limited. (2021). *About us.* https://www.sunpharma.com/
about-us/milestones

Thakkar, K. B., & Billa, G. (2013). *The concept of: Generic drugs and patented
drugs vs. brand name drugs and non-proprietary (generic) name drugs.*
https://www.ncbi.nlm.nih.gov/pmc/articles/PMC3770914/

The Business Tycoons. (2021). *Dilip Shanghvi.* https://www.thebusinesstyco
ons.com/project_sector_rajesh_sanikop_inside_story.php

The New York Times. (2001). *Indian company offers to supply AIDS drugs at
low cost in Africa.* https://www.nytimes.com/2001/02/07/world/indian-
company-offers-to-supply-aids-drugs-at-low-cost-in-africa.html

Torrent Pharma. (2021). *Overview.* https://torrentpharma.com/index.php/
site/info/aboutUs

Ukessays. (2021). *The Indian Pharmaceutical Industry.* https://www.ukessays.
com/essays/economics/the-indian-pharmaceutical-industry-economics-ess
ay.php

USFDA. (2015). *Compliance program guidance manual.* https://www.fda.gov/
media/75201/download

USFDA. (2018). *Generic drug facts.* https://www.fda.gov/drugs/generic-
drugs/generic-drug-facts

WHO. (2011). *Definition of API.* https://www.who.int/medicines/areas/qua
lity_safety/quality_assurance/DefinitionAPI-QAS11-426Rev1-08082011.pdf

Wiki2. (2021). *Cipla.* https://wiki2.org/en/Cipla

Wikipedia. (2021a). *Cipla.* https://en.wikipedia.org/wiki/Cipla.
Wikipedia. (2021b). *Pharmaceutical formulation.* https://en.wikipedia.org/wiki/Pharmaceutical_formulation
Wikipedia. (2021c). *Lupin Limited.* https://en.wikipedia.org/wiki/Lupin_Limited

CHAPTER 3

Marketing Activities of Indian Pharmaceutical Companies

3.1 Marketing and Pharmaceutical Marketing: Meaning and Concept

Marketing always starts with the customer and ends with the customer as they are the valuable assets for any country, and all marketers are very much inclined to deal with them. Marketing is basically a set of business activities by which the goods and products flow of from the manufacturer to the customer (end user), in the light of pharmaceutical marketing, medicines flow from factory to pharmacy. According to Philip Kotler, father of marketing management has defined 'Marketing Management' as 'Marketing is the science and art of exploring, creating, and delivering value to satisfy the needs of a target market at a profit. Marketing identifies unfulfilled needs and desires. It defines measures and quantifies the size of the identified market and the profit potential. It pinpoints which segments the company is capable of serving best and it designs and promotes the appropriate products and services' (Kotler Marketing Group, 2021).

Pharmaceutical Marketing deals with the activities focused on making doctor fraternity as well as the general public aware through the doctor fraternity about the new and existing pharmaceutical brands and make them completely aware about the unique selling propositions (USPs) of the pharmaceutical brand which is promoted to them (Masood et al., 2019).

Pharmaceutical marketing activities are consisting with the following functional areas which are:

a. Providing free samples to the healthcare providers (HCPs).
b. Detailing of product literature/story.
c. Conducting continuing medical education (CME) programmes.
d. Organizing camp activities and support material to patients (end user).
e. Brand promotion through seminars and conferences.
f. Clinical support to patient fraternity through telemedicine and video conferencing.

Pharmaceutical marketing can also be defined as a management process that serves to identify and meet patients' healthcare needs by offering quality and innovative healthcare solution as well as meeting the business objectives (mission and vision) of the organizations.

3.2   Marketing Activities in Indian Pharmaceutical Industry (IPI): An Overview

In India, the activities pertaining to marketing function is being performed in a well-organized manner by the different category of pharmaceutical companies operating in the IPI. Different types of marketing activities help the HCPs to get the most recent update about new medicine launch, addition of new feature in a particular medicine, coverage of indications, side effects wherever applicable, dosage forms, price to the patients (end user), safety, effectiveness and techniques of consuming the medicine (PricewaterhouseCoopers, 2020a, b).

It has been observed that there is an upward trend of demand from the export market due to the capability of pharmaceutical companies of India to produce affordable drugs followed by high degree of efficacy with world-class manufacturing facilities (IBEF, 2021). At the projected scale, this Indian pharmaceutical market (IPM) is comparable to all developed markets, and most of the pharmaceutical companies of India are taking all sorts of proactive measures to provide a world-class healthcare solution to like the other foreign countries such as: China, Japan and US.

There are several factors which are responsible for the growth in Indian pharmaceutical market and the factors are:

- Increasing consumer spending power
- Urbanization
- Healthcare Insurance

Indian pharmaceutical market enjoys a substantial amount of market share of export business. It is said that 'every third tablet sold in the U.S. comes from India'. In the context of the contract research and manufacturing services (CRAMS), India playing a dominant role and gradually emerging as the global hub for many reasons such as:

- Low-cost advantage
- Availability of skilled labour
- Quality and efficacy standards
- Presence of quality pharmacy institutions

Some fundamental changes in marketing strategies of pharmaceutical companies of India have taken place owing to the introduction of product patent in India which has resulted shifting more focus towards innovative medicines backed by research and development (R&D) activities for taking care of the unmet healthcare needs of the patient fraternity (Nandy, 2020; Pal & Nandy, 2019). The major revenue to the Indian Pharmaceutical Industry (IPI) has been gained through exports. India pharmaceutical products are being exported to more than two hundred (200) countries around the world (Bedi et al., 2013). Overall, the marketing function associated with the Indian Pharmaceutical Industry (IPI) helps:

a. To have a healthy competition
b. To increase the customer knowledge
c. To have a better customer relationship
d. To reduce the initial development costs
e. To provide innovative healthcare solution
f. To provide life-saving medicine at an affordable cost
g. To cultivate ethical marketing practices
h. To provide world-class products with unmatched quality and greater efficacy
i. To maintain the proper supply chain

j. To ensure quality healthcare solution to the bottom of the pyramid (BoP)
k. To manage and maintain the value chain both in domestic as well as international front.

3.3   Market Capitalization of Indian Pharmaceutical Industry: Current Context

Today, India is among the top five (5) pharmaceutical emerging markets in the world. Owing to the introduction of GST (Goods and Service Tax) with effect from 1 July 2017, the overall growth of the Indian Pharmaceutical Industry (IPI) has become sluggish followed by transition phase, operational and financial challenges faced by the pharmaceutical companies of India for the financial year 2017–2018, but as per the current predictive market research report is available, the Indian Pharmaceutical Industry (IPI) is expected to grow at a compound annual growth rate (CAGR) of 8–12% during 2018–2021 (Mrinal & Rao, 2019).

From Table 3.1, we can visualize that the total Market Capitalization (as per data availability December 2017) of Indian Pharmaceutical Market. At present, Indian Pharmaceutical Industry (IPI) is currently valued at 116,390 Crores (₹) and growing by 5.5%. We also come to know that there are different therapeutic areas (super group) which are linked to Indian pharmaceutical market (IPM). A graphical representation pertaining to these therapeutic areas (super group) is discussed below.

Figure 3.1 reveals that in Indian pharmaceutical market (IPM), the top three (3) therapeutic (super group) areas are Anti-Infective, Cardiac and Gastrointestinal as far as the current Market Capitalization is concerned. Most of the strategic and proactive pharmaceutical companies of India keep a close eye on the movements of these therapeutic segments (super group) while designing products and formulating the promotional strategies of different branded medicines to ensure the business sustainability. In previous Chapter 2, we have seen that most of the reputed pharmaceutical companies of India operate through multiple divisions; all these divisions are basically designed by keeping the branded medicines connected to a particular therapeutic (super group) for ensuring product promotion in a focused manner to the healthcare providers (HCPs) treating the needy patients with the prescription (Rx)-based therapeutic drug.

Table 3.1 Therapeutic area-wise market capitalization

Therapeutic areas (super group)	MAT Dec-17	
	MAT Dec-17	Gr%
IPM	116,390	5.5
Anti-Infective	16,022	−2.6
Cardiac	14,309	6.7
Gastrointestinal	13,604	6.8
Anti-Diabetic	10,639	14.0
Vitamins/Minerals/Nutrients	10,120	4.2
Respiratory	8695	3.2
Pain/Analgesics	7923	4.1
Neuro/Cns	7413	12.3
Derma	7124	5.7
Gynaecological	5914	5.8
Anti-Neoplastics	2406	4.1
Vaccines	2233	18.2
Opthal/Otoligicals	2200	7.8
Hormones	2027	6.8
Blood Related	1406	6.9
Urology	1389	9.5
Others	1265	7.0
Sex Stimultants/Rejuvenators	640	10.4
Stomatologicals	549	6.3
Anti Malarials	514	−21.9

Source Author's own
Database used AIOCD Pharmasofttech AWACS Pvt. Ltd.

3.4   Manufacturing and Marketing in Indian Pharmaceutical Industry (IPI)

With the homegrown skill and technical know-how, the Indian pharmaceutical marketing companies take 'Manufacturing' of quality medicines with utmost priority for providing the world-class healthcare solution. Most of the reputed pharmaceutical companies of India are having their own manufacturing units or facilities; medium- and small-sized pharmaceutical companies of India manufacture their pharmaceutical products either through third party manufacturers or design their formulation through the contract research organization (CRO). Today, pharmaceutical companies of India are targeting global markets and are becoming more proactive to compete with its global counterparts. India has the tremendous potentiality to establish itself as the design centre by

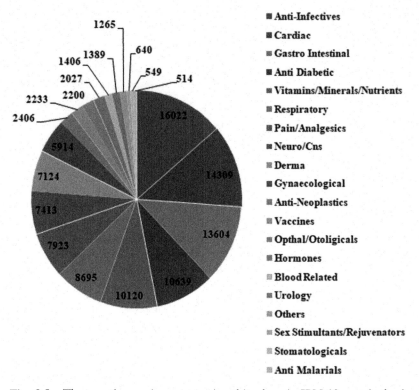

Fig. 3.1 Therapeutic area (super group) and its share in IPM (*Source* Author's own)

providing the intense focus on the design and development of drugs which will enable the pharmaceutical companies of India for the creation of intellectual property rights (IPR). With 'Make in India' initiative in the pharmaceutical sector, Government of India (GoI) is encouraging the existing pharmaceutical companies of India as well as budding entrepreneurs to foster drug innovation and encouraging them from being a powerhouse of low-cost generics manufacturing destination to a research-driven innovation-led biotech manufacturer, and hence most of the pharmaceutical companies of India Nowadays are constantly engaging for skill development as well as building competencies around drug discovery (Pharmalive, 2021).

'Directory of Pharmaceuticals Manufacturing Units in India,' has been brought out by the Department of Pharmaceuticals, Government of India and according to this estimate, 10,563 pharmaceuticals manufacturing units are there in India. The share of top 5 Indian states related to the number of pharmaceuticals manufacturing units is shown in Table 3.2.

From Table 3.2, we can visualize that 5 Indian states, namely Maharashtra, Gujarat, West Bengal, Andhra Pradesh and Tamil Nadu are having the total number of pharmaceutical manufacturing units 3139, 1526, 756, 727 and 570, respectively. The other India states altogether are having 3845 number of pharmaceutical manufacturing units. The percentage (%) of above mentioned Indian states share on total manufacturing units is depicted in Fig. 3.2.

From Fig. 3.2, we can visualize the name of the five (5) Indian states which are playing a crucial role in the area of pharmaceutical manufacturing for catering the healthcare needs of India. From this visual representation, we can also find out that Maharashtra State is holding the highest share of pharmaceutical manufacturing units in India (29.72%). The share of Gujarat, West Bengal, Andhra Pradesh and Tamil Nadu are 14.45, 7.16, 6.88 and 5.40%. The share of 36.40% is contributed by other states of India in the overall manufacturing units of India. The total manufacturing units area is basically consisting with two parameters named as Formulation and Bulk Drugs.

Table 3.2 Top 5 pharmaceutical manufacturing states of India

Sl. No	Name of the Indian state	No. of manufacturing units			% Share
		Formulation	Bulk drugs	Total	
1	Maharashtra	1928	1211	3139	29.72
2	Gujarat	1129	397	1526	14.45
3	West Bengal	694	62	756	7.16
4	Andhra Pradesh	528	199	727	6.88
5	Tamil Nadu	472	98	570	5.40
6	Others	3423	422	3845	36.40
Total		8174	2389	10,563	100

Source Author's own
Database used NPPA, Govt. of India Database Extract
Based on the descending order (highest to lowest) values, the different Indian states have been arranged

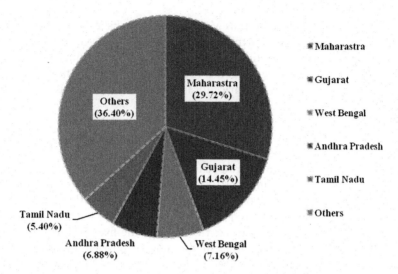

Fig. 3.2 Share of India's top 5 pharmaceutical manufacturing states (The visual representation has been made as per the National Pharmaceutical Pricing Authority (NPPA), Govt. of India Database) (*Source* Author's own)

India's pharmaceutical manufacturing units provide immense impact on the marketing activities of the pharmaceutical companies of India and hence in pharmaceutical Industry of India (IPI), both 'Manufacturing' and 'Marketing' go hand in hand.

3.5   Distribution System and Indian Pharmaceutical Marketing

India is a geographically diverse country with various climate conditions in different states. To fulfil the drug delivery at the right time and at the right place, pharmaceutical companies of India make it mandatory to make all its stock keeping units (SKUs) available at all levels at all times. In the supply chain and drug distribution practices, there was a sea-change observed during 1990. Before this time period, most of the India origin pharmaceutical companies established their own depots and warehouses. But after 1990 and at present, all the company-owned depots and warehouses have been replaced by clearing and forwarding agents (Franchiseindia, 2019).

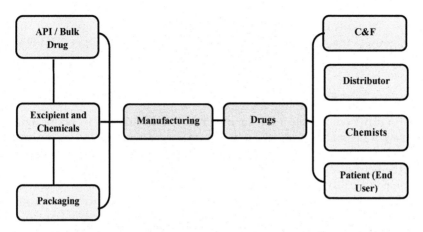

Fig. 3.3 Factory to pharmacy distribution model (*Source* Author's own)

Figure 3.3 depicts how a manufactured product passes through the company-owned central warehouse, which supplies it to the CFA or super-distributor. Stockiest, sub-stockist or hospitals procure the drug products from the CFA. The retail pharmacies procure medicines from the stockist or sub-stockist. With the help of retail pharmacies, finally, the medicine reaches to the needy patients (end user). Certain small manufacturers sometime directly supply the drugs to the CFA. Below, a brief discussion is provided about the important channel components associated with distribution network where most of the Indian pharmaceutical marketing companies provide immense importance (Franchiseindia, 2019).

3.5.1   *Active Pharmaceutical Ingredient/Bulk Drug*

In India, the retailers and the chemists counters enjoy higher margins with generics in comparison to branded drugs. Bulk drugs or APIs are mainly the raw materials which are used to manufacture different formulations, which ensure the shaping of ready-to-use forms of bulk drugs such as: capsules, tablets, syrups and injections) finally administered to patients or end users. Bulk drugs are produced with the combination of by more than two chemicals or intermediaries. They directly create the impact on the diagnosis, cure, treatment, mitigation or prevention of a disease (USFDA, 2021).

3.5.2   Clearing & Forwarding Agents (CFAs)

CFA play a crucial role in Indian pharmaceutical marketing by performing many fold functions like maintaining, storage (stock) of the company's products and forwarding drugs to the stockist or distributors on request, settlement of expiry and breakages to the authorized distributors of the companies, playing different proceedings in the administrative offices for different logistics issues and tax purposes. For better visibility of the products, most of the pharmaceutical companies of India generally keep 1–3 CFAs in each Indian state. On an average, most of the sizeable pharmaceutical companies of India build the network with 25–35 CFAs for taking care of the supply chain needs in pan India basis. The CFAs are being paid by the pharmaceutical companies of India on yearly, once or twice, on a basis of the percentage (%) of total turnover of the products (Dolcera, 2021).

3.5.3   Stockist/Distributor

Authorized distributors or stockists procure stock of company's products from the Clearing and Forwarding Agents (CFAs). Some of the Indian reputed pharmaceutical companies bind the norms as mentioned below for its authorized distributors for the procurement of the company's stocks and compel them to follow the same for proper inventory management and ensuring the flow of capital in a proper and systematic manner (Dolcera, 2021).

Norms for Stockists Order:

$$\{(Sales \times 2.5) - Closing\ Stock - Transit\}$$

The stockists directly place the order to the CFAs, sometime stockists also authorize pharmaceutical company's medical representatives to place the order on their behalf. While working with a particular pharmaceutical company, the same authorized distributor can simultaneously is eligible to work with the other pharmaceutical companies. The credit period of around 10–15 days is given to the city-based distributors, and 21–30 days credit period is offered to the distributors taking care of the supply chain needs in the bottom of the pyramid areas. On the basis of respective Indian pharmaceutical company's norms, a distributor can directly pay to the Company or the CFAs directly. The distributors supply the company's products to the chemists' counters or retail pharmacies where the prescription of the doctors or healthcare providers flows.

3.5.4   *The Retail Pharmacy/Chemists*

The chemists' counters obtain products from the stockist or sub-stockists through whom it finally reaches the consumers/patients/end users. In India, retail pharmacies and chemists are scattered across India. In India, the largest stakeholders of the pharmaceutical supply chain or distributor network are none other than the chemists' counters or retail pharmacies who are the backbone for serving the healthcare needs in the supply chain ecosystem. The healthcare services which are provided by the rural-based chemists counters in the bottom of the pyramid areas by honouring doctors' prescriptions (Rx) followed by making availability of India's top-notch pharmaceutical companies branded medicines are really unmatched (Langer, 2008). Nowadays, the concept of 'pharmacy chain' has also been introduced in India, some of the reputed retail pharmacy chains of India are listed below.

a. Frank Ross Pharmacy
b. Apollo Pharmacy
c. Medplus Pharmacy
d. Sasta Sundar
e. Dhanwantary
f. Life Line

Most of these pharmacy chains are backed by state of the art technology and prove the patient's friendly services by introducing additional service feature 'Online Medicine Stores' where patients/end users and upload the doctors' prescription (Rx) and avail the delivery of the desired medicines in their doorstep.

3.6 Different Marketing Activities and Strategies of Indian Pharmaceutical Companies

International Federation of Pharmaceutical Manufacturers Association (IFPMA) has defined 'pharmaceutical promotion' as: 'any activity undertaken, organized or sponsored by a member company (pharmaceutical company member of IFPMA) which is directed at healthcare professionals to promote the prescription, recommendation, supply, administration or consumption of its pharmaceutical product(s) through all media, including the internet'. According to the World Health Organization (WHO), pharmaceutical product promotion is defined as: 'all informational and persuasive activities by manufacturers and distributors, the effect of which is to induce prescription, supply, purchase and/or use of medicinal drugs' (UK Essays, 2015).

Owing to the fast growth of the pharmaceutical industry, marketing has become a crucial determinant of the sustainable development of various pharmaceutical companies followed by the increasing competition faced by the pharmaceutical companies. The key determinant for defining the success of any pharmaceutical company, besides the cost and availability of capital are brand building. Pharmaceutical companies of India work on monthly, bi-monthly or quarterly promotional cycles; and promotional materials are cautiously assigned to ensure that the company achieves its maximum quantum of sales. Most pharmaceutical marketers formulate the 'strategic framework' which helps to provide the relevant inputs, insights and information on contemporary market competition, approaches to product detailing and a chart on performance-based incentives. Strategies are much more than marketing-plans to achieve the desired business goals and enjoy the competitive advantage in many directions as per the following figure as described (Taylor, 2015).

From Fig. 3.4, we can visualize that pharmaceutical companies of India are attaining different competitive advantage towards different strategies such as: product strategy, product superiority, positioning strategy, manufacturing strategy, distribution strategy, selling skills, field force size, organizational agility, financial strength, selection of product market and target market and competitor analysis by formulating the relevant business strategy to accomplish the desired business objectives. The strategy differs from operational framework because different pharmaceutical companies of India formulate different business strategy based on the business need

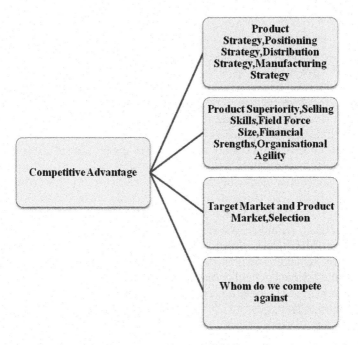

Fig. 3.4 Direction of competitive advantage (*Source* Conceptualized by the Author)

of the organization. The marketing strategies which are incorporated and practiced by different pharmaceutical companies of India and are basically broadly divided into two types as follows:

a. Promotional Strategies
b. Defence Strategies

A brief description about the above mentioned two strategies is discussed below.

I. **Promotional Strategies**

In international context, the Indian Pharmaceutical Industry has been gaining due importance driven by rising consumption levels in the country and strong demand from export markets in the recent time and is expected to move towards an upward trend. The marketing costs being incurred by pharmaceutical companies of India are phenomenal, and all these companies are encompassing the relevant promotional information in an effective manner to the desired audience (IBEF, 2021).

Most of the pharmaceutical companies of India successfully achieved business target in their present business by meeting the healthcare needs of both domestic and foreign customers' and constantly watching the current trends. pharmaceutical companies of India are constantly engaged in creation of new and innovative product promotion ideas as well as searching for opportunities towards increasing market share and profitability and hence deploying adequate expenditure on 'Advertising and Marketing' because this expenditure is directly linked to the financial performance and profitability of the pharmaceutical companies of India (IBEF, 2021). In Indian pharmaceutical marketing, Doctors/HealthCare Providers (HCPs) play a major role in successful execution of different marketing activities executed by different Indian pharmaceutical since the sale of the medicine depends only on prescriptions (Rx) of a doctor. The different marketing activities connected to the successful execution of the 'Promotional Strategies' which are practiced by pharmaceutical companies of India are depicted below.

A. *Direct-to-Consumer Marketing Strategy*

It's is a modern pharmaceutical marketing approach used by the different pharmaceutical companies of India. The reason, for which DTC has gained importance, it is a direct technique of influencing customers who actually consume the medicine. DTC means a marketing communication programme which is intended for targeting consumers or end users. In the context of Indian pharmaceutical product portfolio, the consumers may be patient fraternities, caregivers or the general masses. Initially, Indian doctor fraternities were concerned about the patients struggling to comprehend the drug-related information and insights of doctor/patient relationship, but DTC did not direct to any such anxiety and is now gradually acting as an effective product promotion technique in India. This specific marketing strategy basically functions in the digital platform in India. Internet connectivity in India has totally revitalized direct marketing technique and DTC as a promotional tool (Ventola, 2011).

B. *Right Media Mix Strategy*

'Knowing the valued customer' is one of the biggest challenge and task in front of the pharmaceutical companies of India, and hence pharmaceutical companies of India are creating an integrated marketing campaign based on the marketing research-based data which is enabling pharmaceutical companies of India to be impactful and not get lost in the crowd of competitors have vibrant presence in the market place. Profiling customer's demographics, psychographics and lifestyle market research-based data gets pharmaceutical companies of India started in the right direction to set the correct and contemporary marketing strategy. While formulating the media mix strategy, Indian pharmaceutical marketers closely look upon some important factors like: what kind of demographics? Geography, ethnicity, income, gender and age are just a few of the demographics that impact media choices and buying habits. The right media mix, utilized by the pharmaceutical companies of India, can initiate its product promotion considerably. The various promotional media used by the pharmaceutical companies of India are listed below.

a. Medical Journals and magazines such as: CIMS, Lancet, MIMS, Headache, Physician's Digest, Drug Today, IDR, etc.)
b. Symposium, Conferences and Seminars
c. Promotional endeavours
d. Advertising in the newspapers
e. Providing samples and supplements
f. Conference videos
g. Video contents of conferences and continuing medical education (CME)
h. Clinical Trials
i. Foreign Academic Conferences
j. Professional fees payment for product/brand study

C. *Up-Sell and Cross Sell Strategy*

Some of the brightest Indian pharmaceutical marketers adapt the 'Up-Sell' and 'Cross Sell' promotional strategy and offer extra values at the point of sales slowly and gradually that the other competitors can't match.

D. *Event Management Consultancies (EMCs)*

EMCs are crucial part of marketing strategies. Most of the pharmaceutical companies in India and abroad are nowadays hiring the services of EMCs as part of their marketing strategies and performing brand-building exercises. Event management covers a broad spectrum of brand building-activities from the phase of internal communication to external publicity and also reporting in the financial statements. The major task of EMCs includes: building one-to-one, positive, motivating, effective and self-assuring relationship with the consumer through mass or individual media. It encompasses corporate communication devices, brochures, industry booklets, mailings, catalogues and websites. All these tools have their own distinct features and importance as marketing tools and techniques.

E. *Medico-Marketing*

In Indian pharmaceutical marketing, the purpose of medico-marketing is to plan and promote corporate as well as institutional based health-care services with the active involvement of medical representatives (MRs) and with the help of other direct responsive marketing tools and techniques. The continuing medical education tool has been fruitfully utilized in the medico-marketing. There is a zero-defect planning is required to ensure successful medico-marketing method; crystal clear objective has to be set by meeting the organization's brand promotion objective, high-level professional approach for successful execution of this important task (Docmode, 2020).

F. *Brand Image Marketing*

Pharmaceutical companies of India constantly engage with the brand-building exercises by adapting relevant strategy and techniques for improving the brand image, which in turn improves and ensures the sales and profitability of pharmaceutical companies of India. The following steps are being performed by the pharmaceutical companies of India for the development of the brand image.

Improving Brand Image (8 Steps)

Most of the pharmaceutical companies of India provide emphasis on this promotional strategy to take care of the image of the pharmaceutical brand, and this brand-building exercise of the pharmaceutical companies of India are fulfilled by following all eight steps as mentioned below or a combination of few.

  i. *Launching New Brand*: In this, a small portion of doctors are invited by the pharmaceutical companies of India. The particular drug product features unique selling propositions which are being briefed whenever a new brand is introduced in the market place.
 ii. *Managing Doctor Call*: Time management should be perfectly done as far as doctors' sales call plans are concerned and presentational and product detailing should be brief and concise.
iii. *Evidence-Based Product Promotion*: Product promotion should be executed based on appropriate evidences followed by different tools and techniques such as:

- Case studies followed by success and failure rate
- Clinical Trials of an API or drug-molecule
- Promotional trials of a particular drug-molecule
- Cure rate of drug/medicine
- Side effects of the drug/medicine

All the above mentioned evidence-based promotion-based technique need to be documented properly to ensure a positive perception. Relevant information with appropriate facts and figures always play a greater role in establishing a brand.
 iv. *Coordination and Team Work*: Medical representatives and the concerned reporting managers coordinate each other and should be trained accordingly to create favourable impression in front of the doctor during promotion of the brand.
  v. *Keep it Simple and Short (KISS)*: The relevant information pertaining to a brand should be provided in a simple manner so that doctors will not be overburdened with the information.
 vi. *Identification of Strength of the Brand*: The overall strategy includes advertising or public relations agency managing required activities after identifying the strength of the brand.

vii. *Skill Development*: The development of field staff should take place in a continuous manner to maintain quality standards pertaining to brand promotion.

viii. *Brand Revitalization*: The brand revitalization is a type of specific marketing strategy. It is used when the product reaches to the maturity stage of product life cycle and profits start falling down in a significant manner. Pharmaceutical companies of India provide enormous effort to bring the pharma brand back in the market place to ensure the success to its valued customers.

From Fig. 3.5, we can visualize that pharmaceutical companies of India adapt the brand revitalization strategy by extending brand extension or product lines, addition of new product feature, taking entry to new markets and repositioning the brands. Sometime pharmaceutical companies of India also take into account augmenting the brand, obsoleting or migrating the brand and increasing the frequency of product usages as a part of brand revitalization strategy.

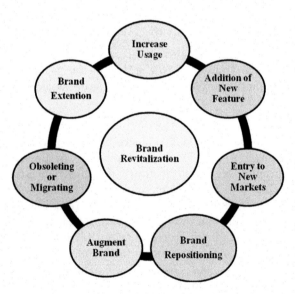

Fig. 3.5 Pharmaceutical brand revitalization strategy (*Source* Author's own)

G. *Involvement Marketing*

In India, there were some baby steps taken for 'involvement marketing' by involving prospective clienteles for promoting some pharmaceutical brands as mentioned below:

- Abdec Drops
- Healthy Baby Contests
- Ferradol's Milkshakes (provided at hospital gatherings) and
- Parke Davis giving away monograms to final year MBBS students at 'specific disease' symposia in medical college in the 1960s.

H. *Innovative Distribution Strategy*

In today's distribution landscape of the Indian Pharmaccutical Industry, pharmaceutical companies are getting intense pressure from every angle. Most of the Indian customers are demanding that distributors should provide value-added services and ensure lower cycle time for ensuring better visibility of the brands. Sometime rebates and discounts are not applicable for higher inventory. Most of the pharmaceutical companies of India, on the other hand, are addressing to the distributors to push inventory and stock, have direct channels to customers and every frequently expressing the willingness to proceed directly to the end users. As a result, the components associated with the supply chain network are witnessing both traditional as well as non-traditional competition.

I. *Co-Marketing*

Co-marketing is a product promotional concept (where two companies collaborate and coordinate on promotional efforts for a co-branded offer for enjoying win–win situation) adopted all over the world; it started before 1970s in India. Co-marketing strategy enables the pharmaceutical companies of India to concentrate on market reach, penetration in the market place and brand share. The final objective of such promotional approach is to develop brand image and brand equity (Sibley, 2020).

J. *Contract Sales Consultants (CSCs)*

Contract Sales Consultants are being considered as one of the important strategic Marketing Tool. Nowadays, most of the pharmaceutical
companies of India are using the services of Contract Sales Consultants
as strategic tool for enhancing the geographical coverage of their product
portfolio and to have a competitive edge at crisis situation.
Benefits of Contract Sales Consultants (CSCs) are:

a. Minimized fixed overheads
b. Increased sales force whenever a specific situation arise like when a
brand is under threat from the competitor
c. Provide creative and innovative, short-term brand resources
d. Managing resources at the launch of new product
e. Assisting in providing market development activities
f. Allow pharmaceutical companies to connect physicians that they are
not are able to call on regular interval by allocating field force and
providing additional sales coverage tailored to a specific need.

K. *Speciality Group Promotion (SGP)*

The marketing strategies of some pharmaceutical companies of India
concentrate on optimizing profits in a focused manner. The pricing
strategy is based at par with the other leading pharmaceutical companies.
The strategy supports a wide range of products to the prescribers, which
has therapeutic coverage.

II. **Defence Strategies**

Defensive strategy is defined as a marketing tool and techniques which
enables pharmaceutical companies of India to take care loyal customers
that can be taken away by its rival competitors. Competitors can be
defined as 'other companies that are situated in the same geography
or market space or sell similar kind of product portfolio to the same
segment of customer base'. When these competitive spirits exist in the
market place, each company must be proactive to protect its own brand,
growth expectations and profitability to maintain a competitive advantage,
adequate reputation among other brands and ensure business sustainability. To reduce the risk of inadequate returns, firms strive to take their
competition away from the industry. Apart from different promotional

strategies, a number of defence strategies have also been incorporated by various pharmaceutical companies of India as a part of their promotional strategy to market, promote and extend the life cycle of their product portfolio. Some of the defence strategies which are generally used in Indian pharmaceutical marketing are depicted and discussed below (Wikipedia, 2021).

A. *New Value Addition (NVA)*

Addition value to an existing product available in the market place ensures further progress of a particular brand. In Indian pharmaceutical marketing, most of the pharmaceutical companies of India adapt this strategy since new indication can widen a product's life as the market exclusiveness period is being extended by three years for each new indication for treating disease and disorders. Often, pharmaceutical companies of India incorporate more vital indications during the launch of the product and less important indications are introduced when product reaches to the decline stage in its life cycle. Sometime New Value Addition to an existing product can act as a differentiation strategy towards generating customer value and protecting the brand imitation as depicted in Fig. 3.6.

B. *Reverse Engineering (RE)*

Reverse Engineering (RE) is a similar type of strategy for gaining new indications or new unique selling propositions (USPs). This strategy

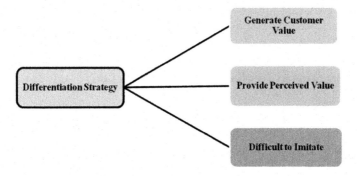

Fig. 3.6 New value addition (NVA) towards differentiation strategy (*Source* Conceptualized by the Author)

is most commonly used where old technology is not viable for business growth and not sustainable. Reverse engineering with the help of 'new technology' can enable the pharmaceutical companies for obtaining satisfactory financial performance.

C. *Brand Switch Control (BSC)*

This strategy is related to two specific subjects which are:

- From: Moving patients from an older drug (whose patent is about to expire)
- To: The newer version (where patent protection is existed).

When generics of the original drug is introduced in the market place after expiry of the patent, then patients which have already switched to a newer drug and are unlikely to switch back to the older and now it has come under the purview of generic drug. Most of the pharmaceutical companies of India nowadays are very much proactive and keeping a close eye on expiry of the existing product patent and developing the product by incorporating the modern technology where the patent is existing for setting the controlling mechanism of brand switch.

D. *Controlling Counterfeit Medicine Mechanism (CCMM)*

Counterfeit medicine is a drug product that is purposely mislabelled with regard to a popular branded drug. These types of medicines can impact the company's goodwill and image, and hence pharmaceutical companies of India are hiring the services of various professional agencies like: 'Pharmaceutical Security Institute' to check and control the grey marketing practices.

E. *Engaging and Enlightening Customers (EEC)*

Most of the pharmaceutical companies of India are shifting towards modern product promotional tools and techniques from the traditional modes of communication and constantly taking endeavour to engage and enlighten customers towards their product portfolio. In earlier days, pharmaceutical companies of India were obsessed with the 'Reach' and 'Frequency' factors since both of these factors are the traditional factors which are used to measure marketing effectiveness and Return on Investment (ROI). 'Reach' is how many 'eyeballs' see the promotional message transmitted by pharmaceutical companies of India, and 'frequency' is how often the consumers see that. Now with the help of modern technology and advent of online marketing-oriented tools and techniques, pharmaceutical companies of India are tracking different e-commerce-based analytics for judging and ensuring the consumer engagement in-depth towards a particular brand being marketed by the pharmaceutical companies of India. Several pharmaceutical companies of India are constantly working to develop a new metric to measure customer engagement in a consistent manner.

F. *Beyond the Pill (BTP)*

Better patient health is the top-most priority of the doctor fraternities. Patients also expect doctors to inform them about services that are beneficial to them to take care of their healthcare needs. Nowadays, pharmaceutical companies of India are taking necessary steps linked to marketing strategy to make doctors' jobs easier and productive by providing quality and contemporary on time services. Most of the pharmaceutical companies of India like Sun, Lupin, Mankind, Cipla and many more are constantly engaged to educate their field force, especially to the medical representatives (MRs) who are happened to be the pillar of the organization for rendering the quality services like:

a. Patient assistance programmes through camp activities.
b. Providing assistance and guidance while dealing with other healthcare stakeholders like *Clinical Health Educators who basically assist doctors in their clinics.*
c. Assist physicians/HCPs in accessing the latest research.
d. *Managing the* enrolment for industry-sponsored Continuing Medical Education courses.
e. *Providing quality assistance pertaining to* new world of *augmented reality, robot-assisted surgeries* and *telemedicine* to the doctor fraternities

Right now, Indian pharmaceutical marketers are constantly cultivating their minds to make the doctor's life as productive as possible by understanding and solving the doctors' pain points for improving healthcare delivery and obtaining satisfactory reciprocation which is directly linked to the financial returns of the pharmaceutical companies of India. Some of the 'beyond the pill' initiatives practices in Indian pharmaceutical marketing space are discussed below with reference to caselets. Nowadays, pharmaceutical companies of India are not only concentration on selling the drugs, rather they all are concentrating for rendering quality healthcare services for improving the healthcare system by conducting different 'beyond the pill' activities as a part of marketing strategy for the service to the mankind not only in local context but also in global perspectives.

REFERENCES

Bedi, N., Bedi, P. M. S., & Sooch, B. S. (2013). Patenting and R&D in Indian pharmaceutical industry: Post-TRIPS scenario. *Journal of Intellectual Property Rights*, *18*(2), 105–110. https://www.researchgate.net/publication/256254 731_Patenting_and_RD_in_Indian_pharmaceutical_industry_Post-TRIPS_sce nario

Docmode. (2020). *Medico marketing going virtual due to COVID-19*. https:// docmode.org/medico-marketing-going-virtual-due-to-covid-19/?utm_sou rce=rss&utm_medium=rss&utm_campaign=medico-marketing-going-virtual-due-to-covid-19

Dolcera. (2021). *Indian pharma industry—Distribution & sales force structure*. http://dolcera.com/wiki/index.php/Indian_Pharma_Industry_-_Distri bution_&_Sales_Force_Structure

Franchiseindia. (2019). *Pharmaceuticals distribution business is an endless opportunity in India*. https://www.franchiseindia.com/wellness/pharmaceuticals-distribution-business-is-an-endless-opportunity-in-india.13659

IBEF. (2021). *Indian pharmaceutical industry*. https://www.ibef.org/industry/ pharmaceutical-india.aspx

Kotler Marketing Group. (2021). *Dr. Philip Kotler answers your questions on marketing*. https://www.kotlermarketing.com/phil_questions.shtml

Langer, E. (2008). *Pharmaceutical distribution in India*. https://www.biopha rminternational.com/view/pharmaceutical-distribution-india

Masood, I., Ibrahim, M., Hassali, M., & Ahmed, M. (2019). Evolution of marketing techniques, adoption in pharmaceutical industry and related issues: A review. *Journal of Clinical and Diagnostic Research*, *3*(6), 1942–1952. https://www.jcdr.net/article_fulltext.asp?id=609

Mrinal, S. K., & Rao, J. (2019). Role of GST in Indian pharma sector. *Open Access Journal of Pharmaceutical Research, 3*(2). https://doi.org/10.23880/oajpr-16000177

Nandy, M. (2020). Is there any impact of R&D on financial performance? Evidence from Indian pharmaceutical companies. *FIIB Business Review, 9*(4), 319–334. https://doi.org/10.1177/2319714520981816

Pal, B., & Nandy, M. (2019). Innovation and business sustainability (IBS): Empirical evidence from Indian pharmaceutical industry (IPI). *Artificial Intelligence for Engineering Design, Analysis and Manufacturing, 33*(2), 117–128. https://doi.org/10.1017/S0890060419000040

Pharmalive. (2021). *Global contract manufacturing companies: Pharmaceutical and biotechnology*. https://www.pharmalive.com/global-contract-manufacturing-companies-pharmaceutical-and-biotechnology/

PWC. (2020a). *Pharma 2020: Marketing the future*. https://www.pwc.com/gx/en/industries/pharmaceuticals-life-sciences/publications/pharma-2020/pharma-2020-marketing-the-future-which-path-will-you-take.html

PWC. (2020b). *Which path will you take?* https://www.pwc.com/gx/en/pharma-life-sciences/pdf/ph2020-marketing.pdf

Sibley, A. (2020). *What is co-marketing? A guide to co-branding marketing campaigns*. https://blog.hubspot.com/blog/tabid/6307/bid/34188/what-in-the-heck-is-co-marketing.aspx

Taylor, D. (2015). The pharmaceutical industry and the future of drug development. *Pharmaceuticals in the Environment*, 1–33. https://doi.org/10.1039/9781782622345-00001. https://pubs.rsc.org/en/content/chapterhtml/2015/bk9781782621898-00001?isbn=978-1-78262-189-8

UK Essays. (2015). *Evolution of marketing techniques in pharmaceutical industry*. https://www.ukessays.com/essays/marketing/evolution-of-marketing-techniques-in-pharmaceutical-industry-marketing-essay.php

USFDA. (2021). *Generic drugs: Questions & answers*. https://www.fda.gov/drugs/questions-answers/generic-drugs-questions-answers

Ventola, C. L. (2011). Direct-to-consumer pharmaceutical advertising: Therapeutic or toxic? *P & T: A Peer-Reviewed Journal for Formulary Management, 36*(10), 669–674. https://www.ncbi.nlm.nih.gov/pmc/articles/PMC3278148/

Wikipedia. (2021). *Defensive strategy (marketing)*. https://en.wikipedia.org/wiki/Defensive_strategy_(marketing)

CHAPTER 4

Research and Development (R&D) Activities of the Indian Pharmaceutical Companies

4.1 Research and Development (R&D) Activities: Definition and Concept

In pharmaceutical industry, R&D can be considered as any activity to resolve scientific uncertainty and unknown targeted at accomplishing an advance in science by answering the unknown for treating different novel diseases or disorders. In pharmaceutical industry, R&D activities are related to the innovative work undertaken on a scientific method for the advancement of knowledge including search of 'new molecular entity' synthesis and modification of known molecules or some methods to boost production rate by adopting different tools and techniques. Pharmaceutical companies utilize R&D to advance its current product portfolio or else bringing 'new chemical entity' through drug discoveries and innovation. In general, pharmaceutical companies want to spend the substantial amount on R&D for bringing new drug and healthcare solution to treat the novel diseases or disorders (Coursehero, 2021; Joseph, 2011; Nandy, 2020; Pal & Nandy, 2019).

4.2   Research and Development (R&D) Process Followed by Indian Pharmaceutical Companies for Developing New Drugs

In India, R&D activities differ from company to company because of the principles and policies of the pharmaceutical companies. The R&D is not performed with the expectation of immediate profit or financial returns. Rather, it is targeted for long-term profitability (Coursehero, 2021; Joseph, 2011; Nandy, 2020; Pal & Nandy, 2019; Pharmabiz, 2011). Pharmaceutical companies that have R&D department try to work out with the new drug discovery and innovation and accordingly allocates substantial amount for the noble cause (Coursehero, 2021; Joseph, 2011; Nandy, 2020; Pal & Nandy, 2019; Pharmabiz, 2011). Pharmaceutical companies always calculate risk while investing in the R&D, risk-adjusted ROI (return on investment) is also taken into the consideration before investing in the pharma R&D and innovation (Coursehero, 2021; Joseph, 2011; Nandy, 2020; Pal & Nandy, 2019). The research-based pharmaceutical companies of India also driven by this basic principle of the business operation. R&D in pharmaceutical sector differs from other commercial activities due to its type of operation (Joseph, 2011). The R&D activities which are performed by the Indian pharmaceutical companies' undergo the multiple phases which are discussed below.

Stage I: Basic Biology
Stage II: Characterization and Target Identification
Stage III: Identification of Hit Compounds
Stage IV: Transforming Hit Compounds to Leads
Stage V: Load Optimization and Reformation
Stage VI: Pre-Clinical Studies
Stage VII: Clinical Study Phase-I
Stage VIII: Clinical Study Phase-II
Stage IX: Clinical Study Phase-III
Stage X: Obtaining Regulatory Approval
Stage XI: Merchandise of Innovative Drug Product

A brief discussion is made in the following pertaining to all the stages (Stage I to Stage XI).

Stage	Clinical trial activities
I to II	Biological studies and examinations are performed to recognize the mechanism of a disease which leads to identification of the particular targets, which plays an important role in treating a specific disease which may be novel in its nature (Joseph, 2011)
III to V	A group of scientists, chemists, biologists and pharmacologists come together in screening and evaluating thousands of compounds, chemically or genetically engineering new ones to generate potential compounds to treat the novel or unknown disease. Those particular molecules that have certain desirable properties are further modified to enhance the activity or minimize side effects. This process is called as 'lead optimization' (Joseph, 2011)
VI	This stage is related to the 'Pre Clinical Activities'. The main objectives of this stage are: • To determine the safe dose for first-in-man study and • Evaluate the innovative product's safety profile Innovative products may include new medical entities, drugs and diagnostic tools or gene therapy solutions. On an average, only one (1) in every five thousand (5000) compounds that reach drug discovery followed by pre-clinical development stage becomes an approved drug (Joseph, 2011)
VII to IX	In these stages, clinical trials (on human element) are conducted to determine the efficacy and safety profile of the molecule. The brief discussion about the clinical trials is made in the following • Phase-I clinical trials are being conducted on a small group of volunteers who are absolutely fit and healthy (human elements) of 20 to 100 to determine the safety profile of the innovative drug (Joseph, 2011) • Phase-II trials involve volunteer who are patients (100 to 500 nos.) and have been suffering with the disease for which drug discovery has been planned. The studies in this phase aim to establish the efficacy of the drug (Joseph, 2011) • Phase-III clinical trials involve a larger group of patient fraternities consisting of 1000 to 5000, and these volunteers are closely monitored at regular intervals to confirm that the drug is effective, working fine in the human body and to identify side effects if any. During the phase III clinical trial studies, toxicity tests and long-term safety evaluations are also evaluated. Clinical trials take approximately 2 to 6 years (Joseph, 2011)

(continued)

(continued)

Stage	Clinical trial activities
X	This stage is related to the regulatory approvals to satisfy the prescribed norms and compliance. The main activities which are performed in this stage are pointed below • Once all the three phases of clinical trials as discussed above are successfully accomplished, the innovative pharmaceutical Indian companies may apply for required regulatory approvals which are compulsory in nature to commercialize the drug (Joseph, 2011) • When a pharmaceutical company in India wants to manufacture/import a novel drug, it has to apply to obtain permission from the licensing competent authority: Drug Controller General of India under the purview of Central Drugs Standard Control Organization by filing in form 44 followed by submitting the data as given in 'Schedule Y of Drugs and Cosmetics Act 1940 and Rules 1945' (Joseph, 2011) • In order to prove safety profile and efficacy to the Indian population, it has to conduct clinical trials in accordance with the guidelines and norms laid down in schedule Y and submit the report of such clinical trials in a prescribed format (Joseph, 2011)
XI	This stage is pertaining to the very important business function which is 'Marketing'. Marketing function is closely connected with the health-care providers and consisting of three main activities which are: (a) Sales activities performed by the pharmaceutical medical representatives (b) Sponsoring in continuing medical education and (c) Providing adequate quantity of drug samples

4.3   NEW CHEMICAL ENTITY (NCE) AND INDIAN PHARMACEUTICAL COMPANIES

According to the U.S. Food and Drug Administration, the definition of a New Chemical Entity is 'a drug that contains no active moiety that has been approved by the FDA in any other application submitted under section 505(b) of the Federal Food, Drug and Cosmetic Act' (Joseph, 2011; Nandy, 2020; Pal & Nandy, 2019). A New Chemical Entity is a molecule developed by the Indian innovative pharmaceutical companies in the early stage of drug discovery stage, which after undergoing subsequent clinical trials could transform into a drug that would be extremely useful for the treatment of some known or novel diseases to cater the contemporary healthcare need. Synthesis of an NCE is the first step in the process of drug development (Joseph, 2011; Nandy, 2020; Pal & Nandy,

2019). Once the synthesis of the NCE has been completed, Indian innovative pharmaceutical companies have two options before them which are.

    a. They can either go for clinical trials on their own or
    b. License the NCE to another pharmaceutical company.

In case of second option, Indian pharmaceutical companies can avoid the lengthy and expensive process of clinical trials, since the licensee pharmaceutical company would be conducting further clinical trials and subsequently launching the drug in the market (Joseph, 2011; Nandy, 2020; Pal & Nandy, 2019). The reason for which some of the Indian pharmaceutical companies adopting 'license the New Chemical Entity to another pharmaceutical company' is this particular model of business would be able to generate high financial returns in the form of different financial performance-related measures like: Return on Assets, Return on Equity, Sales Turnover and Market Capitalization as they get a huge one-time payment for the New Chemical Entity as well as entering into a revenue-sharing agreement with the licensee pharmaceutical company (Joseph, 2011; Nandy, 2020; Pal & Nandy, 2019). Under the 'Food and Drug Administration Amendments Act of 2007', all new chemical entities must first be reviewed by an advisory committee before the U.S. Food and Drug Administration for approving the innovative drug products (Joseph, 2011; Nandy, 2020; Pal & Nandy, 2019). In the following, the list of NMEs which have been developed indigenously by Indian pharmaceutical companies are listed in Table 4.1.

From above-mentioned Table 4.1, we can find the eight indigenously developed novel drugs developed by the different Indian reputed and research-based pharmaceutical companies for the period of 2010–2015. We can also find that two new molecular entities have been developed by BioCon, Sun and Glenmark each and the others NMEs are contributed by India's most reputed pharmaceutical companies: Dr. Reddy's and Primal Life Sciences. Dr. Reddy's anti-diabetic drug, codenamed DRF 2593-307 IN, is the first indigenously developed novel drug to enter phase-III trials.

Table 4.1 List of NMEs developed by Indian pharmaceutical companies (Period: 2010–2015)

Sl. No.	Name of the Indian pharmaceutical company	Name of the NME
1	Biocon	IN-105 (Diabetes-Insulin)
2	Biocon	T1h (Psoriasis & Rheumatoid Arthritis)
3	Dr. Reddy's Lab	DRF 2593-307IN (Diabetes-PPAR Agonists)
4	Glenmark Pharma	Crofelemer (Diarrhoea)
5	Glenmark Pharma	GRC 8200 (Diabetes-DPP IV inhibitor)
6	Primal Life Sciences	P276 (Cancer)
7	Sun Pharmaceutical	Arterolane Maleate + Piperaquine Phosphate (Malaria)
8	Sun Pharmaceutical	Sun-1334H (Allergy)

Source Author's own
Database used Company-wise annual report extract

4.4   Pharmaceutical Research & Development (R&D) Activities in Indian Context

Indian pharmaceutical companies are now focusing on in-house R&D, launching new molecules by their indigenous research capabilities. As a result, research-centric India's pharmaceutical innovative companies have established themselves in various countries including the international market consisting of the developed nations like US and Europe (Coursehero, 2021; Joseph, 2011; Nandy, 2020; Pal & Nandy, 2019; Pharmabiz, 2011). The pharmaceutical companies of India have realized crystal clearly that 'innovation of new drugs' is the way forward for pharmaceutical industry, and hence Indian pharmaceutical companies' are constantly rendering best efforts for conducting different R&D activities like:

- Target identification
- Conducting safety and toxicological studies and
- Lead generation

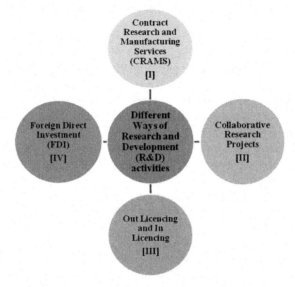

Fig. 4.1 Different ways of R&D activities (*Source* Author's own)

The research-centric pharmaceutical companies of India are rendering best efforts for brining innovation and drug discovery towards ensuring access to affordable medicines and create difference in human life (Pharmabiz, 2011). The most recent R&D practices adopted by the pharmaceutical companies of India in their business model are depicted in the following Fig. 4.1.

A brief discussion about four (I, II, III and IV) ways of R&D activities practiced and performed by Indian pharmaceutical companies are discussed below.

I. *Contract Research and Manufacturing Services (CRAMS)*

CRAMS are essentially outsourcing arrangements. CRAMS include with the following activities.

   a. Manufacturing of Active Pharmaceutical Ingredients and Formulations
   b. Chemistry and Biology Research for New Drug Compounds

c. Pre-Clinical Trials and
d. Clinical Trials

There are many factors forcing multinational companies to outsource their production to India. Cost of manufacturing is substantially low in India—as low as 35% of US costs and 28% of cost in Europe as per the ICRA (an investment information and credit rating agency) report published (Pharmabiz, 2011).

India also has the largest number of US Food and Drug Administration (USFDA)-approved manufacturing plants outside the US. Top global pharmaceutical companies like Pfizer, Merck, GSK, SanofiAventis, Novartis, Teva, etc., largely depend on Indian pharmaceutical companies for the supply of many of their active pharmaceutical ingredients and intermediates (Pharmabiz, 2011).

Foreign companies are very much keen to outsource their production for containing their cost. India has become a favourable destination for many multinational pharmaceutical companies as it has the largest number of USFDA approved plants outside the US (Pharmabiz, 2011).

India has more than 160 FDA approved plants in India, whereas its competitor China has only about 30. In some markets, the drugs will be co-marketed by both companies. In some cases, revenues are shared between Indian and MNCs pharmaceutical companies. A detailed discussion is made in the following with the help of a tabular form pertaining to the various CRAMS activities which take place with the active involvement and engagement of different Indian and MNCs' companies (Pharmabiz, 2011).

From Table 4.2, we can find the list of leading MNC pharmaceutical companies engaged in contract manufacturing with the different pharmaceutical companies of India of repute for developing the drug products and innovative healthcare solution. This is very interesting to note that MNCs are having trust on pharmaceutical companies of India for product development through R&D and CRAMS activities. We can also find different kinds of contract manufacturing tie-ups between Boehringer Ingelheim and Cipla; AstraZeneca and Torrent; Pfizer and Aurobindo; Biocon and Pfizer; and Glenmark is in agreement with Napo pharmaceuticals of US, as part of its collaboration to develop Crofelemer compound for its diarrhoea indication, for the exclusive supply of Napo's global requirement of the API for 'Crofelemer Drug' (Nandy, 2020; Pal & Nandy, 2019).

Table 4.2 Product development through contract research and manufacturing services

Sl. No	Indian company	Multinational company (MNC)	Product development type through CRAMS
1	Lupin Laboratories	Fujisawa Apotex	Cefixime Cefuoxime Cefuroxime Axetil Lisinopril (Bulk)
2	Nicholas Piramal	Allergan Advanced Medical Optics	Bulk & Formulations Eye Products
3	Wockhardt	Ivax	Nizatidine (anti-ulcer)
4	Orchid Chemicals And Pharmaceuticals	Apotex	Cephalosporin and an Injectables
5	Sun Pharma	Eli lilly	CVS Products, Insulin Anti-infective drugs
6	Kopran	Synpac Pharmaceutical	Penicillin-G Bulk Drugs
7	Cadila Healthcare	Atlanta Pharma	Intermediates for Pantoprazole, Gastrointestinal & C Products
8	Biocon	Bristol Myers Squibb	Bulk Drugs
9	Aurobindo Pharma	AstraZeneca, Pfizer	Supply generic medicines for developed & emerging markets
10	Strides Arcolab Limited	Pfizer	Supply 67 generic drugs to Pfizer with focus on Oncology
11	Torrent Pharmaceuticals	AstraZeneca	Supply 18 products for various markets
12	Indoco Remedies	Aspen	Range of Ophthalmic Products for 30 emerging markets
13	Indoco Remedies	Watson Pharmaceuticals	Develop and manufacture generic drugs with market size of US$670 million
14	Cadila Healthcare	Altana, Zyban	Manufacturing of patent drugs
15	Shasun	Eli Lilly, GSK, Novartis	Contract manufacturing for APIs and formulations

(continued)

Table 4.2 (continued)

Sl. No	Indian company	Multinational company (MNC)	Product development type through CRAMS
16	Dishman	Solvay, GSK	Contract manufacturing for APIs and intermediates
17	Jubilant	Novartis	Contract manufacturing for APIs and intermediates
18	Matrix	GSK	Contract manufacturing for API
19	Divi's	MNCs	Custom chemical synthesis
20	Strides Arcolab Limited	GSK	Supply of drugs for semi-regulated markets
21	IPCA	AstraZeneca	Contract generics manufacturing of APIs
22	Torrent Pharmaceuticals	Novo-Nordisk	Contract manufacturing of formulations
23	Strides Arcolab Limited	Mayne, Elilily	Generic Injectables manufacturing
24	Nicholas Piramal	AMO, Allergan	Contract manufacturing for APIs and formulations
25	Sun Pharma	URL Pharma	Contract manufacturing of Generic Formulation
26	Glenmark	Napo	Crofelemer compound for its diarrhoea indication

Source Author's own
Database used Annual reports of different pharmaceutical companies

II. *Collaborative Research Projects (CRPs)*

There is only a thin line differentiating contract drug discovery and development services (CRAMS) and CRPs. The key-points of the differentiation are mentioned in the following.

- In contract drug discovery and development services, the pharmaceutical companies provide discovery services in a number of therapeutic areas, whereas in CRPs, the Indian firm's focus is in the selected therapeutic areas (Nandy, 2020; Pal & Nandy, 2019).
- The pharmaceutical companies may have collaboration with more than one MNC. In CRPs, the MNC and Indian partner jointly discover drug molecules and develop them. In CRPs, unlike in CRAMS, risk is shared proportionally (Nandy, 2020; Pal & Nandy, 2019).
- This would ensure a steady stream of income to pharmaceutical companies of India. Since, the pharmaceutical companies of India work jointly with the MNC pharmaceutical companies, the chances are better for building up specialized skills as compared to CRAMS (Nandy, 2020; Pal & Nandy, 2019).
- The royalty payments are in double-digit percentages and this is a major incentive for pharmaceutical companies of India to enter into CRPs. In the CRPs, Indian company gets upfront payments, milestone and royalty payments depending on the progress and commercialization of the drug (Nandy, 2020; Pal & Nandy, 2019).
- Basically in CRPs, royalty is an extremely essential component of the arrangement, unlike the CRAMS. Some examples pertaining to CRPs given in the following (Nandy, 2020; Pal & Nandy, 2019).

From Table 4.3, we can find the different CRPs between Indian and MNC pharmaceutical companies in different time periods. In 2004, Indian pharmaceutical company Glenmark Pharmaceuticals Limited collaborated with Forest Laboratories (USA) for developing the healthcare solution in the area of Chronic Obstructive Pulmonary Disorder (COPD) and Asthma. Indian pharmaceutical company Piramal Nicholas India Limited engaged with Merck (USA) in the year 2007 for oncology research project. In the year 2009, Indian pharmaceutical company Jubiliant Biosys collaborated with Endo Pharmaceuticals (USA) for developing oncology drugs. We can also find out that there is collaboration in the year 2011 between Serum Institute of India, an Indian pharmaceutical company and Merck (USA) for developing pneumococcal conjugate vaccine. In 2013, Indian pharmaceutical company GVK Bio collaborated with Onconova Therapeutics (USA) for the development of oncology drugs.

Table 4.3 Collaborative research projects (CRPs) in research & development (R&D)

Sl. No	Indian company	Foreign company	Product range	Year of collaboration
1	Glenmark Pharmaceuticals Limited	Forest Laboratories (USA)	Chronic Obstructive Pulmonary Disorder (COPD) and Asthma	September 2004
2	Piramal Nicholas India Limited	Merck (USA)	Oncology	November 2007
3	Jubiliant Biosys	Endo Pharmaceuticals (USA)	Oncology	June 2009
4	Serum Institute of India	Merck (USA)	Pneumococcal conjugate vaccine	August 2011
5	GVK Bio	Onconova Therapeutics (USA)	Oncology	January 2013

Source Author's own
Database used Company-wise annual-report extract

III. *Out-licensing and In-licensing*

All of us are well aware of the fact that discovery and evolution of new drugs require immense financial and monetary resources and expertize, since the R&D activities are very much capital intensive in nature. To obtain the strategic advantage, Indian pharmaceutical companies collaborate with MNCs pharmaceutical companies at the more advanced stages of drug development through subsequent clinical trials and its development. The course of action of R&D takes place with the help and assistance of Out-licensing and In-licensing which have been discussed underneath (Nandy, 2020; Pal & Nandy, 2019).

Out-licensing	In-licensing
Out-licensing is the most widely adopted strategy of major pharmaceutical companies of India. They independently develop the molecule up to a certain stage and then license it out to MNC pharmaceutical companies for further development (Joseph, 2011; Nandy, 2020; Pal & Nandy, 2019). Pharmaceutical companies of India receive upfront and milestone payments and royalty (depending on the terms of the contract), on successful marketing of the drug. Out-licensing has been considered a win–win strategy because on the one hand, it augments the scarcity of resources in finance and research skills of the Indian firms and on the other hand, it gives the MNC pharmaceutical companies access in promising compounds at considerably affordable prices (Joseph, 2011; Nandy, 2020; Pal & Nandy, 2019)	In India, there are also a few cases of in-licensing of molecules for clinical development, though we can find out that these types of in-licensing cases are very few in numbers Example: Indian pharmaceutical company Glenmark has signed an in-licensing deal with San Francisco based Napo Pharmaceuticals for Napo's proprietary anti-diarrhoeal molecule Crofelemer. Diarrhoea is the most commonly reported gastrointestinal symptom in HIV infected patients. About 15–30% of HIV/AIDS infected population is affected with diarrhoea. Napo Pharmaceutical has granted development and commercialization rights to Glenmark in 140 countries including India (outside US, Europe, China and Japan). Glenmark has successfully completed phase-III clinical trials in the US and taking the endeavour for marketing of the drug (Joseph, 2011; Nandy, 2020; Pal & Nandy, 2019)

Source Author's own

IV. *Foreign Direct Investment (FDI)*

Apart from CRAMPs, CRPs, Out-licensing and In-licensing; FDI also playing a significant role in the landscape of R&D in India. FDI is a most important source of non-debt financial resource for the economic development of India (Coursehero, 2021; Joseph, 2011; Nandy, 2020; Pal & Nandy, 2019; Pharmabiz, 2011). The liberalization of FDI has opened the door for outsourcing of clinical trials to India. Foreign companies spend in India to take benefit of relatively lower wages, special investment privileges such as tax exemptions, etc. For an emerging economy like where foreign investments are being made, it also means achieving technical know-how, generating employment and creating sustainable impact on Indian economy (Coursehero, 2021; Joseph, 2011; Nandy, 2020; Pal & Nandy, 2019; Pharmabiz, 2011). The foreign pharmaceutical companies' R&D centres in India claim to do R&D in various therapeutic segments. Some of them like: Pharma Net India Clinical Services, Indus Bio Sciences seem to be actively engaged in the development of processes, delivery systems and derivatives. A large number of R&D investment projects are focused on developing facilities for phase-III clinical trials and other such modules that integrate Indian talent and facilities for conducting developmental work (Coursehero, 2021; Joseph, 2011; Nandy, 2020; Pal & Nandy, 2019; Pharmabiz, 2011). Global pharmaceutical companies are opening their centres in India primarily to take advantage of India's endowment in drug discovery, drug development, clinical trials and also to reap from the innovative capabilities of Indian firms. With the help of FDI, pharmaceutical companies of India and foreign pharmaceutical companies are building their joint collaborations and partnership for development of new drugs on disease areas like cancer, diabetes, malaria and nervous system disorders (Coursehero, 2021; Joseph, 2011; Nandy, 2020; Pal & Nandy, 2019; Pharmabiz, 2011). Some of the examples are provided in the following.

- Dr. Reddy's Laboratories agreement with ClinTec international for joint development of an anti-cancer compound, DRF 1042 (Nandy, 2020; Pal & Nandy, 2019).
- Dr. Reddy's Laboratories (and ClinTec International would co-develop DRF 1042 and also undertake Phase-II and Phase-III clinical trials with the aim of securing US and Europe approvals (Nandy, 2020; Pal & Nandy, 2019).
- Another joint initiative is the Bristol-Myers Squibb Biocon R&D Center (BBRC), which was formed between Syngene International, subsidiary of Biocon and BMS in 2009 for discovery and early drug development (Nandy, 2020; Pal & Nandy, 2019).
- Biocon also has a tie-up with Amylin Pharmaceuticals for developing a peptide drug to treat Diabetes. Both the companies would share the development cost of the drug and would also market the drug jointly in various parts of world depending upon their deal (Nandy, 2020; Pal & Nandy, 2019).

In India, how R&D activities are performed through the route of FDI is depicted in the following with the help of a tabular form.

From Table 4.4, we can find that different MNC pharmaceutical company-wise R&D activities which are continuously taking place in

Table 4.4   R&D activities through the route of foreign direct investment (FDI)

Name of the company		Research & development (R&D) area
Novo Nordisk India Private Limited	a	Insulin analogues—Novomix 30 and Novo Rapid (in 2003)
	b	Insulin Delivery device—Novolet
	c	A third generation durable insulin delivery device—Novopen
Pharma Net India	a	Drug-eluting stents
	b	Implantable drug/device delivery systems
	c	Catheter-based drug-delivery technologies
	d	Co-packaged combination products
Pliva Research India Private Limited	a	Anti-infectives
	b	Cytostatics
	c	Diuretics
	d	Various Api
	e	Nutraceuticals
Roche Scientific Company Limited	a	Transplantation
	b	Oncology
	c	Hepatitis
	d	HIV
Gangagen Biotechnologies Limited	a	Library of over 400 bacteriophages which kill a variety of bacteria present in over 1100 clinical isolates
Indus Bio Sciences Private Limited	a	CarboHydrate Derivatives
	b	Heterocyclic Building Blocks
	c	Reagents and Building Blocks
	d	Chiral Agents and Building Blocks
	e	Nitriles, Acids and Amidines
	f	Pyridines, Piperidines, Pyrimidines & Indazoles
John F. Welch Technology Centre (GE)	a	Improved Diagnostic and Treatment Protocols
Astra Zeneca R&D	a	Cardiovascular
	b	Infection
	c	Neuro Science
	d	Oncology
	e	Respiratory
Merck Development Centre Private Limited	a	Antibiotics
	b	Antimalarials
	c	Cardiologicals
	d	Cough and cold formulations

(continued)

Table 4.4   (continued)

Name of the company		Research & development (R&D) area
	e	Dermatologicals
	f	Haematinics
	g	Neurologicals
	h	ORS
	i	Non-steroidal anti-inflammatory drugs
Novartis India Limited	a	Arthritis and bone metabolism
	b	Cardiovascular and metabolic diseases
	c	Dermatology/Immunopathology
	d	Infectious disease
	e	Nervous system disorders
	f	Oncology
	g	Ophthalmics
	h	Transplantation

Source Author's own
Database used Company-wise annual report extract

Indian soil through the route of FDI. The above evidences indicate that liberalization through the route of FDI has not only resulted in competence building but also created significant impact in R&D activities towards providing novel drug which is also having greater impact for the development of Indian economy and global mankind.

4.5   RESEARCH AND DEVELOPMENT (R&D) ACTIVITIES AND RESEARCH BREAKTHROUGH OF INDIAN PHARMACEUTICAL COMPANIES

There are two types of R&D activities practiced by the pharmaceutical companies of India which are:

a. Basic Research
b. Applied Research

A short description about these two types of researches is made in the following.

'Basic Research' is systematic study aiming at fuller, more complete knowledge and understanding of the fundamental aspects of a concept or a phenomenon (Coursehero, 2021; Joseph, 2011; Nandy, 2020; Pal & Nandy, 2019). Basic research is generally the first step in R&D, performed to give a comprehensive understanding of information without directed applications towards products, policies or operational processes (Coursehero, 2021; Joseph, 2011; Nandy, 2020; Pal & Nandy, 2019). Whereas applied research deals with the scientific study and research activities that seek to solve practical problems which we encounter in our daily lives. These types of research can be used in different ways. For example, it is used to find solutions to healthcare problems, cure illness, and develop innovative technologies to provide healthcare solutions (Coursehero, 2021; Joseph, 2011; Nandy, 2020; Pal & Nandy, 2019). While basic research is time-consuming, applied research is painstaking and more costly due to its detailed and complex nature (Coursehero, 2021; Joseph, 2011; Nandy, 2020; Pal & Nandy, 2019).

India's growing pharmaceutical companies' ability in biology, chemistry, genetics coupled with low-cost clinical trial operability is making India a favoured destination for drug discovery and outsourced R&D (Coursehero, 2021; Joseph, 2011; Nandy, 2020; Pal & Nandy, 2019). This process has improved significantly since 2005, when India completed the formalities of WTO/TRIPS (Trade Related Aspects of Intellectual Property Rights (TRIPs) compliance and norms and started concentrating on product patents (Pal & Nandy, 2019; Pharmabiz, 2011). There are a number of pharmaceutical companies of India who have originated in Indian soil and constantly taking endeavours in various steps of drug discovery and innovation indigenously such as lead generation, target identification and conducting safety and toxicological studies (Coursehero, 2021; Joseph, 2011; Nandy, 2020; Pal & Nandy, 2019). The intense efforts which are being provided in the arena of R&D activities expected that innovation of new drugs is the way forward for pharmaceutical industry (Coursehero, 2021; Joseph, 2011; Nandy, 2020; Pal & Nandy, 2019).

Pharmaceutical companies of India are also investing significantly in drugs that are complex to manufacture such as injectable and biologics. The recent research breakthrough which has taken place in India by conducting different R&D activities are furnished in Table 4.5.

From Table 4.5, we can find two different pictures which are what kind of R&D activities are being performed by pharmaceutical companies of India like Sun, Lupin, Dr. Reddy's, Cipla, Glenmark and Torrent. The second picture which we can find is different outcomes or research break

Table 4.5 Research & development (R&D) activities and research breakthrough

Sl. No	Company name	Research & development (R&D) activities	Research breakthrough
1	Sun Pharmaceutical Industries Limited	Near about 2000 dedicated research scientists employed in multiple R&D centres equipped with cutting-edge enabling technologies for drug discovery and innovation. Scientists those who have expertize in developing generics face difficulty in making technology-intensive products, Active Pharmaceutical Ingredients, Novel Drug Delivery Systems and New Chemical Entities (Pal & Nandy, 2019; Sunpharma, 2021)	Identified and developed arterolane maleate and thereafter was launched in India in 2012 is India's first New Chemical Entity (NCE). The product, Synriam™, has a fixed dose combination of Arterolane maleate 150 mg and Piperaquine phosphate 750 mg is a new age cure for Malaria (Pal & Nandy, 2019; Sunpharma, 2021)
2	Lupin Limited	The combined effort of scientist and respective business teams generate innovative concepts and ideas, exploiting both the unmet market and synergies across therapeutic areas. The company's main focus is on areas like Novel Drug Discovery, complex generics, and Development and Biotechnology (Lupin, 2021; Pal & Nandy, 2019)	A pipeline of 11 highly differentiated and innovative new chemical entities has been developed by the The Novel Drug Discovery and Development team which focuses on therapy areas of CNS disorders, Oncology, Immunology, Pain and Metabolic disorders and a brief description follows (Lupin, 2021; Pal & Nandy, 2019)

Sl. No	Company name	Research & development (R&D) activities	Research breakthrough
3	Dr. Reddy's Laboratories Ltd.	Efforts at the R&D Centre results in a wide-ranging suite of capabilities and services—from synthetic organic chemistry to formulations development; from intellectual property management to regulatory science; from polymorphism to bio-pharmaceutics. For its needy patients, the company is able to offer services and solutions for starting material, intermediates, active ingredients and finished-dosage forms (Dr. Reddy's, 2021; Pal & Nandy, 2019)	170 ANDAs, over 500 DMFs have been obtained by the company and 86 patents filed in the last five years. In March, 2016, Dr. Reddy's Laboratories had entered into a licensing agreement with US-based bio-pharmaceutical company XenoPort to develop and market the latter's clinical-stage oral new chemical entity, XP23829, which is a potential treatment for moderate-to-severe chronic plaque psoriasis and for relapsing forms of multiple sclerosis, in the US market (Dr. Reddy's, 2021; Pal & Nandy, 2019)
4	Cipla Limited	Developing new products is the main focus of the Cipla Research and Development team and thereafter improving existing products as well as drug delivery systems and expanding product applications. Hundreds of scientists work on all facets of pharmaceutical development and technology. The R&D team works with company's strategic partners to file Drug Master Files and Abbreviated New Drug Applications in the US, and seek marketing authorizations in Europe and file product registrations in other jurisdictions (Cipla, 2021; Pal & Nandy, 2019)	The company has obtained near about 100 patents. Patent filing includes drug substances, drug products, platform technologies, IP on polymorphs and crystallinity, and medical devices (Cipla, 2021; Pal & Nandy, 2019)

(continued)

Table 4.5 (continued)

Sl. No	Company name	Research & development (R&D) activities	Research breakthrough
5	Glenmark Pharmaceuticals Limited	Being a central character in the area of drug discovery and innovation, Glenmark has three Research & Development facilities dedicated primarily to drug discovery. In addition, the company has an R&D facility for formulations development & Novel Drug Delivery Systems. The R&D centre at Navi Mumbai, India is focused on discovering NCEs and taking them to the stage of Clinical development. The R&D hub located in Neuchatel, Switzerland is focused on New Biologic Entity research. The third R&D centre, situated in the United Kingdom, focuses on molecules in clinical development for both NCEs and NBEs. The fourth R&D centre at Sinnar, India is focused on developing Specialty/Branded formulations for global markets (Glenmark, 2021; Pal & Nandy, 2019)	The company is having the New Chemical Entity for Compound: GRC 17536, Molecule-TRPA1 Inhibitor indicated for the treatment of Neuropathic Pain and it's on Phase II clinical trial stage. The company is also holding the NME for Compound: GRC 17536, Molecule-TRPA1 Inhibitor, indicated for the treatment of Respiratory Disorders and the clinical trial for phase II already entered (Glenmark, 2021; Pal & Nandy, 2019)

Sl. No	Company name	Research & development (R&D) activities	Research breakthrough
6	Torrent Pharmaceuticals Limited	R&D Centre of Torrent is committed to innovation by discovering novel molecules and formulating unique therapeutic approaches. Torrent's Discovery team has highly motivated and trained scientists evenly distributed between Chemistry and Biology. The focus is on understanding the pathophysiology of the target disease and exploring ways to modulate the disease process. The advantages of being housed in the same campus as the Generic Development team are evident from the seamless integration of the discovery team's efforts into the drug development process needed to ensure smooth transition from the bench to the clinic (Pal & Nandy, 2019; Torrent Pharma, 2021)	Torrent R&D Centre is capable of developing new dosage forms by leveraging company's proprietary technologies such as Dual Retard Inlay Technology, Compact Tablet Technology, Gastro Retentive System and Matrix Based SR/ Modified Release Formulations. Some of the company's novel (first time in the world) solutions are Lamotrigine dispersible-OD formulation and Nicorandil OD formulation to name a few (Pal & Nandy, 2019; Torrent Pharma, 2021)

Source Author's own
Database used Company-wise annual report

through which are the fruit of different R&D activities performed by the India's reputed pharmaceutical companies.

4.6   R&D Infrastructural Development Initiatives of Indian Pharmaceutical Companies

This trend towards development and marketing specialty drugs would be the next step for pharmaceutical companies of India to move ahead in the value chain with good financial returns for ensuring business sustainability (Coursehero, 2021; Joseph, 2011; Nandy, 2020; Pal & Nandy, 2019). There are different pharmaceutical companies of India which are gradually foraying into the field of new drug discovery and innovation (Coursehero, 2021; Joseph, 2011; Nandy, 2020; Pal & Nandy, 2019). A look into the pipeline of these pharmaceutical companies of India shows that most of the pharmaceutical companies of India have already started targeting specific diseases for their drug development and some of the molecules have even reached the phase-III stage clinical trial, and some pharmaceutical companies of India are waiting for regulatory approval for full-fledged commercialization and marketing of the innovative drug. To successfully execute all the important functions, most of the India's innovative pharmaceutical companies are providing more emphasis on the infrastructural development and accordingly taking proactive initiatives (Coursehero, 2021; Joseph, 2011; Nandy, 2020; Pal & Nandy, 2019). Some of the infrastructural development initiatives taken by India's reputed pharmaceutical companies are furnished in Table 4.6.

From Table 4.6, we can find the different R&D infrastructural development initiatives taken by India's reputed pharmaceutical companies.

4.7   Accomplishments Pertaining to Research & Development (R&D) Activities of Different Indian Pharmaceutical Companies

India has a large pool of scientists and chemical engineers who have the potential to take forward the pharmaceutical industry of India to an even higher level, and this R&D task force are constantly dedicating their lives to search for the answer of unanswered questions for providing innovative healthcare solutions for meeting the unmet needs of needy patients by conducting different sorts of R&D activities and performing clinical trials (Pal & Nandy, 2019). Some accomplishments pertaining to the R&D

Table 4.6 R&D infrastructural development initiatives of Indian pharmaceutical companies

Sl. No	Company name	R&D infrastructure development type
1	Alembic Pharmaceuticals Limited	The R&D infrastructure development of Alembic focuses on manufacturing and building facilities for injectable and tablets and also increasing its active pharmaceutical ingredient capabilities (Pal & Nandy, 2019)
2	Divi's Laboratories Limited	Divi Lab has established additional plant in Kakinada in Andhra Pradesh State, India (Pal & Nandy, 2019)
3	Dr. Reddy's Laboratories Ltd.	DRL's capital expenditure with majority of the spending used for biologics and developing information technology and automating processes (Pal & Nandy, 2019)
4	Sun Pharmaceutical Industries Limited	Sun has developed expertize and assembled experience in performing pharmacokinetic and bioequivalence studies to facilitate the introduction of generic or branded generic drugs into the international market (Pal & Nandy, 2019)
5	Lupin Limited	Lupin's dedicated team of scientists and technologists employed at state-of-the art facilities in India and abroad, the company is well on track to evolve as an innovation led transnational pharmaceutical powerhouse providing affordable and economic healthcare solutions with uncompromising quality (Pal & Nandy, 2019)
6	Dr. Reddy's Laboratories Ltd.	The R&D Centre is spread over 300,000 sq. ft. The centre houses over 70 laboratories and has over 800 research scientists working on various projects. This R&D Centre works in close conjunction with other centres across the UK and the Netherlands (Pal & Nandy, 2019)

Source Author's own
Database used Company-wise annual report extract

activities of the pharmaceutical companies of India are mentioned in the following.

a. At present, more than 80% of the antiretroviral drugs used globally to combat Acquired Immune Deficiency Syndrome (AIDS) are being supplied by the pharmaceutical companies of India (Pal & Nandy, 2019).

b. The UN-backed Medicines Patent Pool has signed six sub-licences with different reputed and globally recognized pharmaceutical companies of India Cipla, Emcure, Laurus Labs, Aurobindo, Desano and Hetero Labs which have enabled them to make generic anti-AIDS medicine TenofovirAlafenamide (TAF) for 112 developing countries (Pal & Nandy, 2019).

c. Some of the reputed and well-regarded pharmaceutical companies of India have been continuously receiving satisfactory number of Abbreviated New Drug Application approvals from the USFDA. India accounts for around 30% (by volume) and about 10% (value) in the US$70–80 billion US generics market as far as the current market research data is available (Pal & Nandy, 2019).

d. Pharmaceutical companies of India are also investing significantly in drugs that are complex to manufacture such as injectable and biologics. Some of the very recent research breakthrough which has performed in India is furnished in the following Table 4.7.

Table 4.7 Innovative drugs of Biocon

Sl. No	Company name	Brand name	Brand's unique selling proposition (USP)	Indications
1	Biocon	Biomab EGFR	Biocon's first indigenously developed monoclonal antibody which has reached the market	Head & Neck cancer
2	Biocon	Anti-CD6	It helps to develop antibody for autoimmune diseases	Autoimmune Diseases like Psoriasis

Source Author's own
Database used Biocon's annual report extract

4.8   RESEARCH AND DEVELOPMENT (R&D) SPENDING OF FIVE REPUTED INDIAN PHARMACEUTICAL COMPANIES: A COMPARATIVE ANALYSIS (F.Y. 2010 VERSUS F.Y. 2017)

Besides building on the traditional generic product portfolio and pipeline, pharmaceutical companies of India are now investing adequate amount in R&D on complex generics, specialty and differentiated products, and biosimilars. The strong financial balance sheets of India's reputed pharmaceutical companies allow them to make such capital-intensive investments on a sustainable basis for the cause of R&D activities as well as conducting clinical trials which are most critical and crucial part of R&D activities. In the following, a table pertaining to the R&D spending of five reputed pharmaceutical companies of India along with the comparative analysis (F.Y. 2010 versus F.Y. 2017) is presented in Table 4.8.

From the above mentioned Table 4.8, we can find that the India's most reputed pharmaceutical companies together have spent a record Rs 8025 (₹) crore in R&D activities during the F.Y. 2017–2018. The R&D expenditure constitutes 9% of the cumulative revenues of the India's five (5) reputed pharmaceutical companies. The total R&D expenditure for the most reputed Indian five (5) pharmaceutical companies has increased six-fold since F.Y. 2010.

4.9   COMPARATIVE ANALYSIS OF RESEARCH AND DEVELOPMENT (R&D) EXPENDITURE BETWEEN INDIAN AND FOREIGN PHARMACEUTICAL COMPANIES (PERIOD: 1995–2015)

Nowadays, pharmaceutical companies of India are taking the proactive measures for providing the quality healthcare solutions for treating different diseases and disorders. India's reputed pharmaceutical companies also are successfully filing ANDAs (abbreviated new drug application) to USFDA for the review and potential approval of a generic drug product and getting satisfactory approvals from USFDA (Coursehero, 2021; Joseph, 2011; Nandy, 2020; Pal & Nandy, 2019). After obtaining the regulatory approval, reputed and research-based pharmaceutical companies of India manufacture and market the innovative drug product to ensure a safe, effective, quality and affordable healthcare solution for improving human lives. India's R&D-centric pharmaceutical companies now appear to match their global counterparts in investing for the

Table 4.8 R&D spending comparative analysis: period F.Y. 2010 versus F.Y. 2017

Companies	F.Y. 2010				F.Y. 2017			
	R&D spend	Revenues	R&D spend as % of revenue	Net profit	R&D spend	Revenues	R&D spend as % of revenue	Net profit
Sun Pharma	208.2	3808.6	5.5	1351.1	2145.8	30,264.2	7.1	6964.3
Lupin	343.8	4773.6	7.2	681.6	2310	17,119.8	13.5	2557.4
Aurobindo Pharma	97.2	3575.4	2.7	563.4	543	14,844.7	3.7	2301.6
Cipla	228.1	5359.5	4.3	1082.5	1071	14,280.8	7.5	1006.3
Dr. Reddy's Labs	379.3	7027.7	5.4	106.7	1955	14,080.9	13.9	1257.2
Total	1256.6	24,588.4	5.1	3785.3	8024.8	90,590.4	8.9	14,086.8

Source Author's own
Database used Company-wise Annual Report Extract
Amount in: INR Crores (₹)

future by transforming their traditional business model into R&D-centric business model. A comparative analysis pertaining to R&D expenditure between Indian and MNCs pharmaceutical companies is illustrated below for the study period (Coursehero, 2021; Joseph, 2011; Nandy, 2020; Pal & Nandy, 2019).

From Table 4.9, we can find the R&D expenditure of Indian and Multinational pharmaceutical companies for the study period 1995–2015. We can also find out the percentage (%) of change pertaining to the

Table 4.9 Comparative analysis of R&D expenditure (Period: 1995–2015)

Year	A Total R&D (in $ million)	B Domestic R&D (in $ million)	C Foreign R&D (in $ million)	D Domestic R&D (% change)	E Foreign R&D (% change)
1995	30.46	19.16	11.3	62.90	37.10
1996	33.89	20.8	13.09	61.38	38.62
1997	36.72	22.67	14.05	61.74	38.26
1998	38.88	24.05	14.83	61.86	38.14
1999	40.82	25.32	15.50	62.03	37.97
2000	58.27	39.80	18.47	68.30	31.70
2001	71.60	54.17	17.43	75.66	24.34
2002	96.35	76.53	19.82	79.43	20.57
2003	134.37	91.68	42.69	68.23	31.77
2004	226.69	160.94	65.75	71.00	29.00
2005	326.15	233.48	92.67	71.59	28.41
2006	423.11	293.98	129.13	69.48	30.52
2007	547.22	422.65	124.57	77.24	22.76
2008	641.49	489.45	152.04	76.30	23.70
2009	613.89	474.66	139.17	77.32	22.68
2010	799.16	622.72	176.44	77.92	22.08
2011	959.84	773.66	186.18	80.60	19.40
2012	959.96	794.67	165.29	82.78	17.22
2013	1045.23	869.25	175.98	83.16	16.84
2014	1134.61	956.17	178.44	84.27	15.73
2015	1142.86	965.82	181.35	84.51	15.49

Source Author's own
Database used Prowess Database, Centre for Monitoring Indian Economy
Total R&D (in $ million) in Column A = Summation of Column B and Column C
Domestic R&D (% change) in Column D = Column B / Column A × 100
Foreign R&D (% change) in Column E = Column C / Column A × 100

R&D expenditure in case of both Indian and Multinational pharmaceutical companies for the study period. This evidences also indicate that the R&D costs which are being invested by the India's pharmaceutical companies are to compete with their global counterparts such as Teva, Mylan and Allergan for gaining the competitive advantage in long run and trying hard to be at par with these MNCs as far as R&D expenditures are concerned for providing innovative healthcare solution. In the following, a Trend Analysis is presented with the help of the dataset presented in Table 4.9.

From Fig. 4.2 and Table 4.10, we can find the movement of R&D expenditures as 'Total R&D Expenditure (in \$ million)', 'Domestic (India) R&D Expenditure (in \$ million)' and 'Foreign (MNC) R&D Expenditure (in \$ million)' over the study period followed by three (3) different trend lines representing Model-I, II and III separately. In the X axis, we can find the 'Year' pertaining to the study period, and in Y axis, we can find the 'R&D Expenditure (in \$ million)'

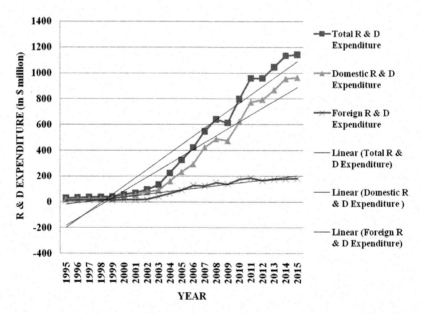

Fig. 4.2 Trend analysis of research and development (R&D) expenditure of domestic (Indian) and foreign (MNC) pharmaceutical companies (Period: 1995–2015) (*Source* Author's own. *Software used* Microsoft Excel [Version-2010])

Table 4.10 Trend line interpretation of R&D expenditure

Model No.	Model name	Trend/regression type	Equation	R Square (R^2)
I	Total R&D Expenditure (in $ million)	Linear	$y = 64.40x - 262.6$	0.922
II	Domestic R&D Expenditure (in $ million)	Linear	$y = 53.47x - 234.2$	0.908
III	Foreign R&D Expenditure (in $ million)	Linear	$y = 10.99x - 28.78$	0.911

Source Author's own
Software used Microsoft Excel (Version-2010)

being incurred by domestic (Indian) and foreign (MNC) pharmaceutical companies. A regression analysis of our dataset incorporated in the Model-I, Model-II and Model-III provide the equation of the trend line as $y = 64.40x - 262.6$, $y = 53.47x - 234.2$, and $y = 10.99x - 28.78$, respectively. We can further observe that the slope of the trend line is upward in case of all the models followed by R^2 value as 0.922, 0.908 and 0.911 for Model-I, II and III, respectively, which further explains that 92.20% in case of Model-I, 90.80% in case of Model-II and 91.10% in case of Model-III of the variance of the dataset incorporated in our study has been explained by the 3 different liner trend lines. In case of Model-III, we can find that the linear trend line is relatively flatter which indicates that the R&D expenditure of foreign (MNC) pharmaceutical companies is not that much adequate in Indian context; but we have observed that there is a continuous spending of R&D expenditure incurred by foreign (MNC) companies for the study period. In Model-II, we can find an upward liner trend line pertaining to the R&D expenditure in Indian drug and pharmaceutical sector for the study period and the reason of this upward trend line may be due to the some important factors which are high-level inclination for innovation of pharmaceutical companies of India, paradigm shift in the business model from me-too drug product category to innovative healthcare solution, deploying substantial amount of funding (10–15% of the revenue in some cases) for the innovation of drug and pharmaceutical products by the pharmaceutical companies of India, availability of scientific workers and quality raw materials.

References

Cipla. (2021). *Manufacturing.* https://www.cipla.com/about-us/manufactu
ring

Coursehero. (2021). *What is 'research and development—R&D'?* https://www.
coursehero.com/file/31834600/Self-assessmentdocx/

Dr. Reddy's. (2021). *Research and development.* https://www.drreddys.com/net
herlands/dr-reddy-s-research-and-development/

Glenmark. (2021). *R&D centres.* http://www.glenmarkpharma.com/novel-mol
ecular-entities/rd-centres

Joseph, R. K. (2011). *The R&D scenario in Indian pharmaceutical industry.*
http://ris.org.in/images/RIS_images/pdf/dp176_pap.pdf

Lupin. (2021). *Research.* https://www.lupin.com/research/

Nandy, M. (2020). Is There any impact of R&D on financial performance?
Evidence from Indian pharmaceutical companies. *FIIB Business Review, 9*(4),
319–334. https://doi.org/10.1177/2319714520981816

Pal, B., & Nandy, M. (2019). Innovation and business sustainability (IBS):
Empirical evidence from Indian pharmaceutical industry (IPI). *Artificial Intelligence for Engineering Design, Analysis and Manufacturing, 33*(2), 117–128.
https://doi.org/10.1017/S0890060419000040

Torrent Pharma. (2021). *R&D Centre.* https://torrentpharma.com/index.php/
site/info/rnd

Pharmabiz. (2011). *R&D activities in Indian pharma sector.* http://www.pha
rmabiz.com/PrintArticle.aspx?aid=61832&sid=0

Sunpharma. (2021). *Research and development.* https://sunpharma.com/operat
ions/research-and-development

CHAPTER 5

Global Competitiveness of Pharmaceutical Industry of India: Trends and Strategies

5.1 GLOBAL COMPETITIVENESS: MEANING AND CONCEPT

'Global Competitiveness' is the combination of two words: 'Global' and 'Competitiveness' (Global + Competitiveness). The word 'Global' basically relates to the whole world or worldwide. Competitiveness can be defined as 'the capacity to provide products and services as or more effectively and efficiently than the pertinent competitors. In the traded sector, this means sustained success in international or global markets without protection or subsidies' (Busru & Singh, 2017).

According to the Global Competitiveness Report (GCR) published by the World Economic Forum (WEF) for 2017–2018, India ranks 40th position out of 137 Nations' economies (Busru & Singh, 2017). The ranking of BRICS (Brazil, Russia, India, China and South Africa) nations are provided in the following.

From Table 5.1, we can visualize that India's rank is 40 as per the Global Competitiveness Report (GCR) published by the World Economic Forum (WEF) (Busru & Singh, 2017). According to this WEF's report, India as a country is enjoying a global competiveness followed by a satisfactory global competitiveness ranking and several parameters such as institutions, macroeconomic environment, infrastructure, health and basic education, quality higher education and training, labour market

© The Author(s), under exclusive license to Springer Nature Singapore Pte Ltd. 2022
M. Nandy, *Relationship between R&D and Financial Performance in Indian Pharmaceutical Industry*,
https://doi.org/10.1007/978-981-16-6921-7_5

Table 5.1 Ranking of BRICS nations

Name of the country (BRICS nations)	World Economic Forum (WEF) ranking
China (C)	27
Russia (R)	38
India (I)	40
South Africa (S)	61
Brazil (B)	80

Note The BRICS WEF ranking has been mentioned based on the ascending order
Source Author's own
Data Source World Economic Forum

capability, financial market development, goods market capability, technological readiness, market size, business sophistication and innovation. These parameters act as 12 important pillars to take India to the greater heights (Karnani, 2012; Nandy, 2020; Pal & Nandy, 2019).

5.2 GLOBAL PHARMACEUTICAL INDUSTRY (GPI): CURRENT SCENARIO AND TRENDS

The Global Pharmaceutical Industry (GPI) is accountable for the drug product development, production and marketing of healthcare solutions throughout the world. Thus, it creates the global healthcare needs. The Global Pharmaceutical Industry (GPI) is constantly developing at an extraordinary speed. International pharmaceutical manufacturing companies are facing tremendous challenges owing to new medicines and therapy forms, changing regulations and progressing digitization, high market growth (Contractpharma, 2018).

The global pharmaceutical market is growing persistently. Increase in urbanization and a growing middle class are making drugs available and economical for people at large and lead to a higher demand for medication for speedy recovery from different diseases and disorders (Contractpharma, 2018). Moreover, the emergence of new viruses, pandemics and drug-resistant infections drive towards significant R&D activities, revenue supplying pharmaceutical manufacturers proposition from more products in their product portfolio and pipelines (Busru & Singh, 2017).

Apart from all the above-mentioned factors, life expectancies are gradually growing up of many global citizens and hence they are expressing their keen interests towards purchasing quality medicines to enhance their quality of life and happiness by getting recovered from the different diseases and disorders. Groundbreaking changes are occurring in the area of biological agents and prescription (Rx)-based biosimilar drugs, for instance regarding the autoimmune diseases, treatment of cancer, as well as rare illnesses which affect a very small group of patients worldwide (Contractpharma, 2018; Karnani, 2012).

Global Pharmaceutical Industry (GPI) posted consistent growth during the period of 2007–2017 and the same is presented in the following.

From Table 5.2, we can visualize the global pharmaceutical sales (in billion British pounds) for the period of 2007–2017. We can find out that in the year 2007 the Global Pharmaceutical Sales (in billion British pounds) were 329 billion British pounds and the sales have grown in a consistent manner. After ten (10) years, i.e. in 2017, the Global Pharmaceutical Sales (GPS) have been reported as 738 billion British pounds followed by the upward sales trend. The trend of Global Pharmaceutical Sales (in billion British pounds) for the period of 2007–2017 are illustrated in Fig. 5.1 based on the dataset presented in Table 5.2.

From Fig. 5.1, we can visualize the trend line pertaining to Global Pharmaceutical Sales (GPS in billion British pounds) for the period of 2007–2017. In the horizontal (X) axis, 'Year' has been plotted, and in the

Table 5.2 Global pharmaceutical sales (GPS) (Period: 2007–2017)

Year	Global pharmaceutical sales (billion British pounds)
2007	329
2008	366
2009	468
2010	481
2011	503
2012	516
2013	511
2014	393
2015	605
2016	648
2017	738

Source Author's own
Data Source North American Industry Classification System (NAICS)

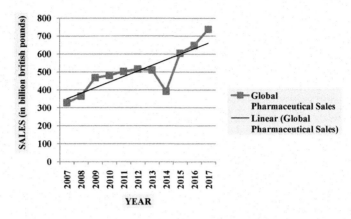

Fig. 5.1 Trend of global pharmaceutical sales (in billion British pounds) (Period: 2007–2017) (*Source* Author's own. *Software used* Microsoft Excel [version 2010])

Table 5.3 Trend line interpretation of global pharmaceutical sales

Model no	Model name	Trend/regression type	Equation	R^2
I	Global Pharmaceutical Sales from 2007 to 2017 (in billion British pounds)	Linear	$y = 31.05x + 318.9$	$R^2 = 0.708$

Source Author's own
Software used Microsoft Excel (version 2010)

vertical (Y) axis, we can find the Global Pharmaceutical Sales in billion British pounds. In Table 5.3, we can find a regression analysis of our dataset incorporated in Model-I which provides the equation of the trend line as $y = 31.05x + 318.9$. We can further observe that the slope of the trend line is upward followed by R^2 value 0.708 which explains that 70.80% of the variance of the dataset incorporated in our study has been explained by the liner trend line which is upward in nature for the period of 2007–2017 and this upward trend may be because more global pharmaceutical manufacturers are extremely eager to serve five major emerging national economies: Brazil, Russia, India, China and South Africa which all together acronym as 'BRICS', and hence, the revenue of Global Pharmaceutical Industry (GPI) is expected to grow, international pharmaceutical drug manufacturers are targeting different region-specific diseases which result in global consumer demand for high-margin biologic drugs. The upward global sales trend may be due to increase in population and a growing middle class in emerging economies, boosting demand for both brand name and biosimilar prescription (Rx)-based products, and globally, more individuals over the age of 65 require healthcare solution to treat their different chronic illnesses which result in demand for industry products.

5.3 Role of Pharmaceutical Industry of India (IPI) in the Context of Global Pharmaceutical Market (GPM)

India's contribution to global health care has spanned across the realms of alternative medicine starting with Ayurveda and Yoga, age-old health traditions. Important contribution of India to global health care, however, is made by its drugs and pharmaceutical sector. Indian medicines are found in almost every country across the globe. Pharmaceutical companies in India develop and manufacture quality healthcare formulations for most of the countries in the world and also make active pharmaceutical ingredients (API) for other global pharmaceutical companies. These quality drugs are in demand all over the world. In addition, pharmaceutical companies of India offer different healthcare solutions and services which are associated with the development of new drugs including clinical trials.

Biosimilar and other innovative medicines are also increasingly becoming active in the field. Indian generics account for 20(%) of global exports in terms of volume as India is the largest provider of generic drugs globally, and hence, pharmaceutical industry of India is named as 'pharmacy of the world'. Pharmaceutical companies of India are constantly engaged with new product launches for meeting the contemporary healthcare needs across the global. In the following, a list of new product launch (Indian pharmaceutical company-wise) is provided.

From Table 5.4, we can visualize the list of new product launch of different pharmaceutical companies of India as well as few subsidiaries

Table 5.4 List of new product launch (Indian pharmaceutical company-wise) (Period: 2009–2018)

Sl. No	Indian pharmaceutical company	Name of the new drug product with indication	Year of launch
1	Sun Pharma	Anti-fungal powder Abzorb as prescription & OTC product	April 30, 2018
2	Hikma Pharmaceuticals	Palonosetron Hydrochloride Injection	April 3, 2018
3	Hetero Pharma	Generic FDC combo of 'emtricitabine & tenofovir alafenamide'	February 27, 2018
4	Natco Pharma	Generic version of tenofovir alafenamide (TAF) 25 mg used for the treatment of hepatitis B	December 20, 2017
5	Glenmark Pharmaceuticals Limited	Nicotine replacement therapy, Kwitz in India	November 16, 2017
6	Lupin LTD	Bupropion hydrochloride extended release tablets USP (XL), 150 mg and 300 mg having received an approval from the US FDA	June 15, 2017
7	Ozone Ayurvedics	ITIS plus care eye drops—The herbal nutritional eye lubricant for soothing relief to dry, tired & irritated eyes	May 23, 2017
8	Mankind Pharma	Anti-hypertensive-drug Zolahart (Azilsartan)	May 17, 2017
9	Dr Reddy's Laboratories	Generic version of sofosbuvir 400 mg and velpatasvir 100 mg fixed-dose combination, indicated for the treatment of chronic hepatitis C, under a brand name Resof Total, in India	May 15, 2017
10	Sanofi-Synthelabo India Private Limited	Two drugs for type 2 diabetes patients in India: Lyxumia (lixisenatide) and Zemiglo (gemigliptin). Lyxumia is a once daily, non-insulin injectable drug and Zemiglo is a once daily, oral tablet	July 19, 2016
11	Hetero Pharma	Biosimilar 'Bevacizumab' in India for the treatment of metastatic colorectal cancer (mcrc) under the brand name 'Cizumab'	June 27, 2016

Sl. No	Indian pharmaceutical company	Name of the new drug product with indication	Year of launch
12	Cipla Ltd	Ledipasvir-sofosbuvir in India under the brand name Hepcvir-L. Hepcvir- L, the first once-a-day, fixed-dose oral combination therapy that has been approved for chronic hepatitis C genotype 1 patients	December 21, 2015
		Low-dose HIV drug Efavirenz 400 mg	December 1, 2015
13	Dabur India	Ratnaprash sugarfree specially to help fight fatigue	December 9, 2015
14	Mission Pharmacal	Hycofenix (hydrocodone bitartrate, pseudoephedrine hydrochloride, and guaifenesin) oral solution. Hycofenix effectively relieves three cough and cold symptoms in just one prescription	November 20, 2015
15	Novalead Pharma	Galnobax- a topical gel for treatment of diabetic foot ulcer (DFU)	November 4, 2015
16	Dr. Reddy's	Nise D spray, emphasizing its strategic intent of being a player of substance in the Indian over the counter (OTC) space. Nise D spray offers quick and targeted pain killing	November 2, 2015
17	Zydus PHARMA	Sovihep' which will provides succour to more than 10 million patients who suffer from hepatitis C in India	March 17, 2015
18	Reckitt Benckiser	The third generation advance antifungal cream contains terbinafine- an antifungal agent that is faster, more effective and reduces the chances of the infection returning	July 22, 2014
19	GVK Biosciences	'CLINOGENT' for innovative solutions	July 16, 2014
20	Dr Reddy's Laboratories	Melgain for treatment of vitiligo	June 12, 2014
21	OSIM India	Anti-stress head massager ucrown2	May 28, 2014

(continued)

Table 5.4 (continued)

Sl. No	Indian pharmaceutical company	Name of the new drug product with indication	Year of launch
22	Dr Reddy's Laboratories Ltd	Moxifloxacin hydrochloride tablets 400 mg, a therapeutic equivalent generic version of Avelox (moxifloxacin hcl) tablets 400 mg in the US market	March 5, 2014
23	Dr Reddy's Laboratories Ltd	Sumatriptan injection USP, autoinjector system 6 mg/0.5 ml, for subcutaneous use, a therapeutic equivalent generic version of Imitrex statdose Pen (sumatriptan succinate) 6 mg/0.5 ml	February 26, 2014
24	Mylan Pharmaceuticals Private Limited	Hertraz is indicated for the treatment of HER2-positive metastatic breast cancer and is available in two strengths, 440 mg and 150 mg	February 4, 2014
25	Dr Reddy's Laboratories Ltd	Sildenafil tablets (20 mg), a bioequivalent generic version of Revatio tablets	November 19, 2012
26	Sagent Pharmaceuticals	Caffeine citrate injection and oral solution	October 6, 2012
27	Wockhardt Ltd	15 mg and 30 mg delayed release capsules of lansoprazole, which is used in treatment of peptic ulcers	September 17, 2012
28	Cipla Ltd	'Qvir', a novel 4 drug kit for treating HIV/AIDS	August 14, 2012
29	Elder Pharmaceutical	Combe launch Vagisil range of feminine personal hygiene products	February 27, 2012
30	Lupin	Launches generic Keppra tablets in US	September 14, 2011
31	Himalaya Drug	Launches Liv.52 HB to treat hepatitis B virus	May 5, 2011
32	Themis Medicare	Launches new cosmeto dermatology product Lumixyl	February 22, 2011
33	Dr Reddy's Lab	Launches zfirlukast tablets in US markets	November 22, 2010
34	Strides Arcolab	Launches Starflu in retail for anti H1N1	September 25, 2009
35	Troikaa Pharma	Launches Xynova Endo for customized endoscopy procedures	September 22, 2009

Source Author's own
Data Source Year-Wise Company-Wise Annual Reports

of multinational pharmaceutical companies operating in India for the period of 2009–2018. We can also find out that most of the pharmaceutical companies of India have launched successfully innovative healthcare solution to cater the healthcare need both in domestic and international front.

Reputed pharmaceutical companies of India like Sun, Glenmark, Lupin, Dr. Reddy's, Elder, Himalayan and many more are launching different new drugs in a continuous manner during the study period for the treatment of different diseases and disorders.

5.3.1   Current Position of India in Global Export Value

Like India, there are many other foreign countries like Germany, Canada, Switzerland, Italy also participate in the global export process of drug and pharmaceutical products. Over the last decade, in an ever-evolving global pharmaceutical landscape, India has shown the way with cost-competitiveness and has led the way with generics. Today with increasing cut throat competition, pharmaceutical companies of India are moving into the speciality generics business. The world is now looking for affordable drugs and India has been continuously delivering the same. In the following, we will come to know where India lies among the other global countries participating regularly in the pharmaceutical export process.

From Table 5.5, we can visualize that 86% export (total 100%—other countries 14%) of global pharmaceutical market (GPM) solely depends on 15 different countries. From this table, we can find out that Germany contributes highest (16%) medicines exports. Canada's contribution is 1.60% in the world's pharmaceutical exports. India has performed well in comparison with other foreign countries like Spain, Sweden, Austria and Canada by contributing 2.60% drug and medicine exports and grabbed 11th position as far as the top 15 countries' drug and medicine exports in 2017 (by %) are concerned. In the landscape of global pharmaceutical exports, India has obtained satisfactory position and it may be due to the ability in providing high-quality medicines backed by strong innovation capabilities and a structural cost advantage.

Table 5.5 Country-wise export value for F.Y. 2017–2018 and India's rank

Sl. No	Country name	Total global drugs/medicines exports share (%)
1	Germany	16
2	Switzerland	12.50
3	Belgium	8.10
4	France	7.40
5	United Kingdom	6.20
6	United States	6.10
7	Italy	5.60
8	Netherlands	5.40
9	Ireland	5.20
10	Denmark	3.40
11	**India**	**2.60**
12	Spain	2.30
13	Sweden	1.90
14	Austria	1.60
15	Canada	1.60
16	Other Countries	14
	Total	**100**

Source Author's own
Data Source International Trade Centre (ITC) and World Trade Organization (WTO)

5.3.2   Therapeutic Area-wise Export Share of Pharmaceutical Industry of India (IPI)

The pharmaceutical industry of India has achieved immense importance and established itself in the global pharmaceutical domain. In today's world, science-based IPI ranks 11th in terms of export contributed in the global pharmaceutical market. The pharmaceutical companies of India nowadays dominate the global pharmaceutical market which was earlier traditionally managed by multinational pharmaceutical companies. The product portfolio of the pharmaceutical industry of India ranges from simple headache pills to the sophisticated antibiotics and also complex cardiac compound; for example, it might be anything like formulations, bulk drugs, generics, novel drug delivery system, new chemical entities or biotechnology.

In the following, we will come to know about the therapeutic areas which IPI caters as well as their respective contribution on overall export value of IPI.

From Table 5.6, we can find out that India supplies different kinds

Table 5.6 Therapeutic area-wise export share of pharmaceutical industry of India (IPI)

Product	Global market share (Therapeutic Area-wise) (%)
Anti-infectives	16
Cardiovascular	13
Gastro Intestinal	11
Vitamins, Minerals	8
Respiratory	9
Pain/analgesic	7
Anti-diabetic	7
Others	29
Total	**100**

Source Author's own
Data Source IMS Health Database Extract

of finished dose formulations pertaining to anti-infectives, cardiovascular, gastrointestinal, anti-diabetic and many more therapeutic solutions for treating different diseases. Figure 5.2 has been made based on the dataset presented in Table 5.6. From Fig. 5.5, we can visualize that India enjoys the highest export share, i.e. 16% in case of anti-infective drugs. The therapeutic areas where India enjoys more than 10% export share in its overall exports are cardiovascular (13%) and gastrointestinal (11%). We can also find out that India's drug and pharmaceutical exports are not only restricted in a particular therapeutic area; rather, pharmaceutical industry of India is extremely dedicated to cover up various world's diseases and accordingly manufacture and market the healthcare solution in the different international countries and it may be because major Indian pharmaceutical companies and medical suppliers including Ajanta Pharma, Bafna Pharmaceuticals, Aurobindo Pharma, Cipla, Cadila Pharma, FDC, Mylan Labs, Piramal Enterprises, Simaxo Chemicals, Sun Pharma Industries export various kinds of healthcare solutions to the different international countries and have been playing a major role in attaining the top position.

5.3.3 Country-wise Drug and Pharmaceutical Product Export of India

Around 175 countries which include the highly regulated markets of the US, the European Union (EU) and Australia, the semi-regulated markets

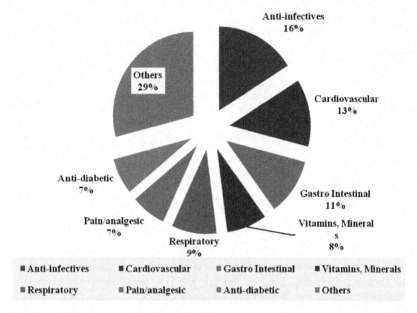

Fig. 5.2 Therapeutic area-wise export share of pharmaceutical industry of India (IPI) (*Source* Author's own. *Software used* Microsoft Excel [version 2010])

of Singapore, Taiwan, Brazil, etc., to markets of lower regulation such as Sri Lanka and African countries, the drug and pharmaceutical exports of pharmaceutical industry of India are destined (Karnani, 2012; Nandy, 2020; Pal & Nandy, 2019). The relative strength and competencies of pharmaceutical companies of India are in producing high-quality generic and innovative products as the bulk of India's export of pharmaceutical products is destined towards the US and other European nations. In the following, we will come to know how pharmaceutical industry of India promotes the sustainable healthcare development in the vital field of medicines by manufacturing quality drug and pharmaceutical products and export the same across different nations in the world.

From Table 5.7, we can visualize that India serves different nations across the globe by providing quality drug and medicinal products as well as offering healthcare solution. We can also find out that maximum export (in US$ billion/million) which India caters worldwide is in US consisting with 3.8 US$ billion which is extremely significant and occupy 32.90%

Table 5.7 Drug and pharmaceutical product export of India (country-wise)

Rank	Country	Value	US$ billion/million	Share (%)
1	United States	3.8	Billion	32.90
2	South Africa	461.1	Million	3.90
3	Russia	447.9	Million	3.80
4	United Kingdom	444.9	Million	3.80
5	Nigeria	385.4	Million	3.30
6	Kenya	233.9	Million	2
7	Tanzania	225.2	Million	1.90
8	Brazil	212.7	Million	1.80
9	Australia	182.1	Million	1.60
10	Germany	178.8	Million	1.50
			Total =	56.50

Source Author's own
Data Source Export Promotion Council of India

India's total exports to different nations. The reason for the highest percentage (%) export in US may be due to pharmaceutical companies of India always comply with USFDA stringent norms while manufacturing the different drug and pharmaceutical products. India has large number of USFDA-approved manufacturing plants, and USFDA competent authorities inspect all plants which are approved by USFDA and would like to ensure whether desired quality standards are being met or not before importing to US. Satisfying USFDA stringent norms and meeting its protocol and compliances result adequate amount of US export business of pharmaceutical companies of India. Apart from US, Indian drug and pharmaceutical exports are also made to other foreign countries like South Africa, Kenya, Brazil, UK, Germany and many more. We also come to know that more than 50% of India's drug and pharmaceutical exports are to these 10 countries. Apart from US, pharmaceutical companies of India export its higher percentage (%) drugs and exports to South Africa, Russia, UK and Nigeria and the share in total drug and export (country-wise) is 3.90 US$ million, 3.80 US$ million, 3.80 US$ million and 3.30 US$ million, respectively.

5.4   Current Trends of Important Parameters of Pharmaceutical Industry of India (IPI)

Developed countries' (US, UK) global pharmaceutical market has recognized India's role as the main contributor to the lowering of healthcare costs. Different reputed Western non-governmental organizations as well as foundations such as the Bill and Melinda Gates Foundation; Doctors without Borders; and the Clinton Foundation procure Indian drug and pharmaceutical products for use in their healthcare work in Africa. Apart from the developed nations, pharmaceutical companies of India are also supplying drug and pharmaceutical products to different developing economies with affordable medicines and helping to provide the quality medicines to cure the different diseases. The Indian pharmaceutical sector is constantly becoming stronger and is making a difference across the world and hence becomes the 'backbone of health care' in the different nations. For example, 40% of generic drugs prescribed (Rx) in the US are from India and all these drugs are inclusive of research-intensive, innovative anti-cancer medications and biosimilar drugs (Karnani, 2012; Nandy, 2020; Pal & Nandy, 2019). There are certain important parameters which share the pharmaceutical industry of India to compete in the global front and the trends of these important parameters of pharmaceutical industry of India are discussed one by one in the following.

a. Export Performance Trend of Pharmaceutical industry of India.
b. Abbreviated New Drug Application Filing Trend at U.S.F.D.A.
c. Drug Master Filing Trend at U.S.F.D.A.

5.4.1   Current Trend of Drugs and Pharmaceutical Export of Pharmaceutical Industry of India (IPI)

The future looks even progressive as because the export of pharmaceutical industry of India is growing steadily. With very less challenges and huge opportunities for the Indian pharmaceutical reputed companies, the export performance is definitely going to create significant value for their further business expansion and growth.

Pharmaceutical companies of India keep up the innovation in the forefront and becoming more aggressive to stay ahead of its international competitors like China.

Low-cost, large-scale manufacturing capability, second highest number of US FDA-approved facilities and culture of innovation and faster technology adoption are creating significant influence in the export performance for many pharmaceutical companies of India.

In the following, we will come to know the drug and pharmaceutical export performance trend of pharmaceutical industry of India for the study period (Table 5.8).

From Table 5.9, we can visualize the Export Performance of Indian Drug and Pharmaceutical Products for the study period (1995–2015). Figure 5.3 has been made based on the dataset presented in Table 5.9. The trend line interpretation has been presented in Table 5.9. From Fig. 5.6, we can visualize the 'Year' in the horizontal (X) axis and 'Export

Table 5.8 Export performance of Indian drug and pharmaceutical products (Period: 1995–2015)

Year	Drug & pharmaceutical export of India	Year	Drug & pharmaceutical export of India
1995	660	2006	3184.02
1996	672	2007	4159.44
1997	780.49	2008	5078.77
1998	729.76	2009	5191.18
1999	855.91	2010	6676.43
2000	945.1	2011	8483.46
2001	1055.74	2012	10,062.7
2002	1400.77	2013	11,140.5
2003	1620.07	2014	6826.09
2004	2061.66	2015	6488.4
2005	2444.17		

Source Author's own *Amount in US$ million.*
Data Source Ministry of Commerce and Industry, Government of India

Table 5.9 Drug and pharmaceutical export of India trend line interpretation

Model no	Model name	Trend/regression type	Equation	R^2
I	Drug and Pharmaceutical Export of India	Linear	$y = 480.6x - 1452$	$R^2 = 0.802$

Source Author's own
Software used Microsoft Excel (version 2010)

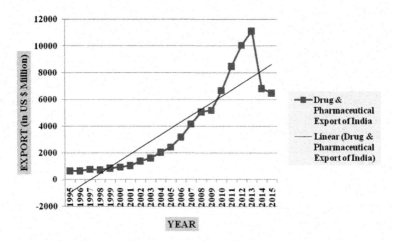

Fig. 5.3 Export performance trend analysis of Indian drug and pharmaceutical products (Period: 1995–2015) (*Source* Author's own. *Software used* Microsoft Excel [version 2010])

(in US$ Million)' of Indian drug and pharmaceutical products in vertical (Y) axis for the study period. A regression analysis of our dataset incorporated in the Model-I provides the equation of the trend line as $y = 480.6x - 1452$. We can further observe that the slope of the trend line is upward followed by R^2 value 0.802 which further explains that 80.20% of the variance of the dataset incorporated in our study has been explained by the liner trend line. The upward trend pertaining to Indian drug and pharmaceutical products for the study period may be due to the some important factors which are availability of good quality raw material, skilled workforce, low cost of innovation, extensive supply chain network, professionally managed technicians and pharma professionals proficient with English language and manufacturing compliance and documentation as per norms of different countries.

5.4.2   Current Trend of Abbreviated New Drug Application (ANDA)

Abbreviated New Drug Application (ANDA) contains data which is submitted or applied to United States Food and Drug Administration (USFDA) for the review and potential approval of a generic drug product once approved; an applicant may manufacture and market the generic drug product to provide a safe and secure, effective, lower cost alternative to the brand name drug it references.

Generic drug product can be defined as one that is equivalent as well as can be compared to an innovator drug product in dosage form, route of administration, strength, performance, quality, characteristics and intended use.

Most of the time Indian pharmaceutical manufacturers manage to secure the satisfactory number of ANDA approvals from USFDA regulatory authority which translate into higher revenues for them once they start marketing their approved generic products in the US. In the following table, Abbreviated New Drug Application (ANDA) Filing at USFDA for the study period is provided.

From Table 5.10, we can find out the ANDA Filing Dataset at United States Food and Drug Administration (USFDA) which has been submitted by the different pharmaceutical manufacturers of India. On the basis of this dataset, a trend line is presented in the following.

From Fig. 5.4, we can visualize the trend line of Abbreviated New Drug Application (ANDA) Filing at USFDA for the study period (1995–2015). In the horizontal (X) axis, 'Year' has been plotted, and in vertical (Y) axis, Abbreviated New Drug Application, i.e. ANDA (in numbers) Filing at USFDA, has been mentioned. We can figure out that the liner trend line has covered up and connected all the data points and taken an

Table 5.10 Abbreviated new drug application (ANDA) filing at USFDA (Period: 1995–2015)

Year	No of ANDA filings	Year	No of ANDA filings
1995	3	2006	274
1996	6	2007	302
1997	17	2008	342
1998	20	2009	345
1999	22	2010	353
2000	32	2011	392
2001	43	2012	400
2002	59	2013	420
2003	104	2014	430
2004	167	2015	450
2005	247		

Source Author's own
Data Source USFDA

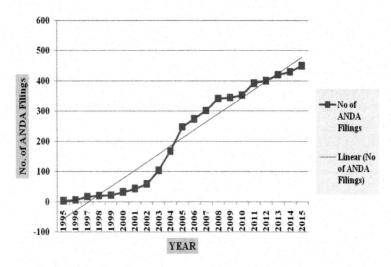

Fig. 5.4 Trend line of abbreviated new drug application (ANDA) Filing at USFDA (Period: 1995–2015) (*Source* Author's own. *Software used* Microsoft Excel [version 2010])

upward shape. The further interpretation of the upward liner trend line has been provided in Table 5.11 where we can find a regression analysis of our dataset incorporated in the Model-I which provides the equation of the trend line as $y = 26.69x - 82.78$. We can further observe that the slope of the trend line is upward followed by R^2 value 0.949 which further explains that 94.90% of the variance of the dataset incorporated in our study has been explained by the liner trend line which is upward in nature. The liner trend line is becoming upward due to filing ANDA by various reputed pharmaceutical companies of India at USFDA in a

Table 5.11 ANDA filings trend line interpretation

Model no	Model name	Trend/ regression type	Equation	R^2
I	No. of ANDA Filings	Linear	$y = 26.69x - 82.78$	$R^2 = 0.949$

Source Author's own
Software used Microsoft Excel (version 2010)

continuous manner as a result in the year 2017 the highest number of ANDA approvals has been obtained by the Indian pharmaceutical manufacturing companies. Among the pharmaceutical companies of India, the Zydus group and its subsidiaries secured 77 approvals. The Zydus group is followed by Aurobindo Pharma (51), Sun Pharma (22) Glenmark Pharmaceutical (18), Lupin (17), Gland Pharma (16), Alkem Laboratories (15), Macleods Pharma (15), Cipla (10) and Dr Reddy's (10) ANDA approvals in the year 2017. The other relevant reasons of the upward trend of ANDA Filings Trend line are: most of the reputed pharmaceutical companies of India nowadays concentrate more on complex generics and speciality products to maximize margin and ensure adequate return on investment (ROI) and their ANDA Filings at USFDA remaining stronger day by day; in front of pharmaceutical companies of India, ANDA Filings at USFDA mainly act as an innovation and speciality business which ensures more financial returns, and hence, lot of emphasis is given on ANDA Filings to enjoy the global competeness.

5.4.3   Current Trend of Drug Master File (DMF)

Drug Master File (DMF) is generally submitted to the USFDA that is used to provide confidential as well as detailed information about processes, facilities, or articles used in the manufacturing, processing, storing of drugs and packaging. DMFs are meant to support abbreviated new drug applications (ANDA), which are used to register generics at USFDA. DMFs are basically filed for supplying active pharmaceutical ingredient or bulk drugs.

India continues to lead in the number of drug master files filed with the USFDA and the same we will come to know from the following table.

From Table 5.12, we can visualize the submission of Drug Master Filings (DMFs) by different pharmaceutical companies of India for the study period. From this table, we can find out that greater (>) than 300 DMFs at USFDA have been registered from the year 2007 and the DMF trend is upward. On the basis of the dataset as presented above, a trend line of DMFs is presented in the following for the study period.

In Fig. 5.5, we can visualize the trend line of Drug Master Filings submitted by pharmaceutical companies of India at USFDA for our study period. In the horizontal (X), 'Year' has been plotted, and in the vertical

Table 5.12 Drug master filings (DMF) at USFDA (Period: 1995–2015)

Year	No. of DMF filings	Year	No. of DMF filings
1995	4	2006	277
1996	6	2007	309
1997	17	2008	350
1998	20	2009	347
1999	23	2010	351
2000	33	2011	354
2001	43	2012	355
2002	59	2013	356
2003	103	2014	358
2004	164	2015	362
2005	247		

Source Author's own
Data Source U.S.F.D.A

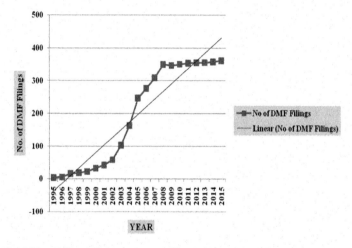

Fig. 5.5 Trend line of drug master filings (DMF) at USFDA (Period: 1995–2015) (*Source* Author's own. *Software used* Microsoft Excel [version 2010])

(Y) axis DMFs (in numbers) have been represented. We can further visualize that the liner trend line has connected all the data points of our incorporated dataset and taken an upward shape.

In Table 5.13, we can find a regression analysis of our dataset incorporated in the Model-I which provides the equation of the trend line

Table 5.13 DMF trend line interpretation

Model No	Model name	Trend/ regression Type	Equation	R^2
I	No. of DMF filings	Linear	$y = 23.37x - 60.02$	$R^2 = 0.901$

Source Author's own
Software used Microsoft Excel (version 2010)

as $y = 23.37x - 60.02$. We can further observe that the slope of the trend line is upward followed by R^2 value 0.901 which explains that 90.10% of the variance of the dataset incorporated in our study has been explained by the liner trend line which is upward in nature. The liner trend line of Drug Master Filings is in the upward direction because most of the pharmaceutical companies of India are concentrating well on the R&D activities for providing the innovative healthcare solutions. From the perspective of the 'me-too' product portfolio, research-based and reputed pharmaceutical companies of India are constantly engaging with Novel Drugs Discovery System. With this endeavour and efforts, pharmaceutical companies of India increase their competencies for filing the DMFs in continuous manner at USFDA and enjoying the global competeness over other countries in the global pharmaceutical market. Most of the innovative pharmaceutical companies consider both generics and patented drug market while formulating their DMF business strategy (Karnani, 2012; Nandy, 2020; Pal & Nandy, 2019).

5.5 Strategies Pertaining to Global Competitiveness of Pharmaceutical Industry of India (IPI)

For many decades, the pharmaceutical companies of India have been exporting various medicines to different nations across the globe followed by different unprecedented challenges. For example, every country has its own norms and regulations as far as medicinal imports are concerned, in case of some specific country's stringent norms and regulations; the export performance of different pharmaceutical companies of India sometime slows down. But this is encouraging to note that with fewer challenges pharmaceutical companies of India have been successfully providing quality medicines and serving the mankind globally for treating different ailments and the pharmaceutical exports of India are constantly growing in a significant way and adding value to the overall growth of the national gross domestic product. In front of the global pharmaceutical market, pharmaceutical industry of India has been recognized as 'Pharmacy of the World', 'Pharmacy of the Developing Economies' and 'Backbone of the Nations' since a satisfactory percentage (%) of world's drug and pharmaceutical products are being supplied by pharmaceutical companies of India. India's strong position as a drug and pharmaceutical global pharma supplier rests on some strategies. The strategies which are closely linked and associated for taking India in the greater heights and gaining the worldwide competitive advantage in serving and managing the global pharmaceutical supply chain are illustrated in the following with the help of relevant examples (Fig. 5.6).

A. Affordable Pricing Strategy (APS)

The first and foremost strategy which pharmaceutical industry of India adopts is 'Affordable Pricing Strategy (APS)'. Under the purview of this strategy, IPI can provide the quality drugs and pharmaceutical products as well as healthcare solution across the globe with an affordable price and compete with its global counterparts. In global pharmaceutical market (GPM), pharmaceutical companies of India can offer quality medicines with lesser price owing to low-cost operations since India's cost of production in case of drugs and pharmaceutical products is nearly 33% lower than that of the US and 30–40% lower than other comparative pharmaceutical manufacturing hubs such as China and Eastern Europe. Some of the advantages and accomplishments which pharmaceutical industry of India has achieved by utilizing 'Affordable Pricing Strategy (APS)' are stated in the following.

I. The largest provider of generic drugs globally accounting for 20(%) of global exports in terms of volume by the pharmaceutical industry of India.

II. Pharmaceutical companies of India export economical generic drugs to the Latin American, in contrast to the costly, patented products supplied by the multinational companies (Kiran & Mishra, 2009). This has shown Latin American governments and people to have a positive view of India as an important contributor

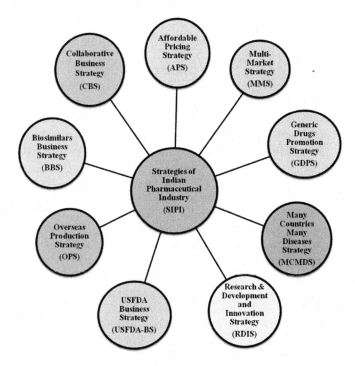

Fig. 5.6 Strategies of Pharmaceutical Industry of India (SIPI). *Note* SIPI Figure has been conceptualized based on the strategies pertaining to global competitiveness practiced by the pharmaceutical companies of India during the study period (*Source* Author's own)

to their objective to reduce the cost of health care. This is encouraging to note that both Chile and Brazil have motivated the entry of pharmaceutical companies of India into their respective countries to put pressure on multinational pharmaceutical companies (MNCs) and local drug-makers to increase the visibility of generics and affordable medicines (Viswanathan, 2017).

III. Developing countries' essential medicines that are used in 70–90% are manufactured in India. For example:

a. UNICEF sources developing countries 50% of its medicines from India (Sapra, 2016).

b. India has provided 80% of the AIDS treatment drugs that Doctor without Borders issues in over 30 countries (Sapra, 2016).

c. Biocon, India's largest biotech company, is focused on delivering affordable innovation in the domain of biosimilar drugs. The company is also performed to decrease chronic therapy costs of immunological disorders like cancer, diabetes and autoimmune diseases by leveraging India's cost advantage to deliver affordable healthcare solutions to the patient fraternities across the globe (Sapra, 2016).

d. The discovery of new molecules, both NCEs (new chemical entity) and NBEs (new biological entity). Mumbai-based Glenmark Pharmaceuticals Ltd is playing a leading role. Branded generics markets across emerging economies the company has a significant presence (Sapra, 2016).

e. Torrent Pharma, the flagship company of Torrent Group, is ranked among the top pharma companies of India. The company has been recognized as a dominant player in the therapeutic areas of central nervous system (CNS) and cardiovascular (CV). This reputed pharmaceutical company has achieved significant presence in gastrointestinal, anti-infective, diabetology and pain management segments in the global pharmaceutical market (GPM) (Sapra, 2016).

f. India-based Cadila Pharmaceuticals Ltd is one of the largest privately held pharmaceutical companies. The company has been actively involved in developing and manufacturing quality pharmaceutical products in India and marketing its quality drug product portfolio over eighty-five (85) countries around the world from the last six decades (Sapra, 2016).

g. Cipla is a globally recognized and reputed Indian pharmaceutical company whose business objective is 'ensuring no patient across the world shall be denied access to high quality & affordable medicine and support'. This objective itself indicates the social cause Cipla's business policy which is not only applicable in Indian context but the same is also applicable in global context (Sapra, 2016).

h. Pharmaceutical companies of India are also recognized as the biggest suppliers of low-cost vaccines across the world. For example, we can state that 'Serum Institute of India Private

Limited' is the world's largest vaccine manufacturer. Annually Serum produces and sells approximately 1.3 billion vaccine doses across the globe. The vaccine doses are consisting of different life-saving vaccines like the Polio vaccine as well as Diphtheria, Pertussis, Tetanus Hib, r-Hepatitis B, Measles, BCG, Mumps, and Rubella vaccines (Sapra, 2016).

i. The recombinant Hepatitis B vaccine is an excellent example of one of India's low-cost medicines offered for the service to the needy people at large. Large multinational pharmaceutical companies had been enjoying a high-level monopoly on the vaccine followed by exorbitant pricing. Surprisingly India saw an unmet healthcare need in this particular domain and, owing to the absence of patent barriers; developed a high-quality Hepatitis B vaccine to reduce the price of the drug and finally started offering the drug as less than $1 per dose which was earlier $23 per dose offered by the MNCs. Today, India is a main and major supplier of vaccines to UNICEF (United Nations Children's Emergency Fund) and to the Ministries of Health of various countries across the globe (Sapra, 2016).

B. Multi-Market Strategy (MMS)

To get the global competitive advantage in global pharmaceutical market (IPM), most of the pharmaceutical companies of India adopt 'Multi-Market Strategy (MMS)'. While adopting this business strategy, pharmaceutical companies of India take both 'Regulated Global Pharmaceutical Market (r-GPM)' like North America (US), Europe, South Africa, Australia, Japan, China, Korea, and Taiwan and 'Un-Regulated Global Pharmaceutical Market (ur-GPM)' consisting with Latin America, South America (Brazil), Some African Countries, Asian group, CIS (common wealth of Independent states) countries into the consideration and supply the quality medicines to cater the healthcare demand (depicted in Fig. 5.7).

Regulated market exporting is tough because it involves high cost in maintaining good manufacturing practices (GMP) and quality standards at par with global norms. Less number of pharmaceutical companies has adequate resources to undertake such activity. India's top domestic companies like Sun Pharmaceuticals, Dr. Reddy's Laboratory, Cadila,

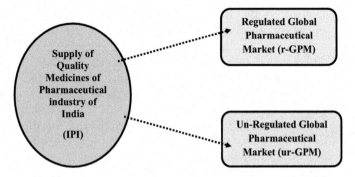

Fig. 5.7 Multi-market strategy (MMS) of pharmaceutical industry of India (*Source* Author's own)

Cipla and Lupin Laboratory and few medium-sized companies like Ipca Labratories, Neuland Laboratory, Alembic Limited and a few others have targeted the global regulated market (Khare, 2014). Pharmaceutical companies of India in large proportions (about 40%) are exporting their products in the semi-regulated or unregulated market like BRICS economies, Asian and African countries. Unregulated market advantage of exporting is that there is lesser of an entry barrier and very low technological base production.

C. Generic Drugs Promotion Strategy (GDPS)

India is currently the largest provider of generic drugs to global markets. Nearly 5% each in the top 10 generic drug markets Indian pharmaceutical export consumption has been in US, UK, Russia, etc., for the year 2013 and the same is predicted to rise year on year (Gupta, 2018). Indian pharmaceutical generic drug use is also increasing in other nations like Canada, France, Germany, Brazil and Japan. Indian generic drugs globally with the Indian generics account for 20% of global exports in terms of volume and this percentage is set to rise over the coming years (Gupta, 2018).

D. Many Countries Many Diseases Strategy (MCMDS)

The most crucial business development strategy which is being adopted by pharmaceutical companies of India is 'Many Countries and Many

Diseases Strategy (MCMDS)' to explore the business opportunities across the globe for managing the supply chain across many countries by targeting the country-wise diseases and disorders. By understanding the country-wise different diseases and disorder, pharmaceutical companies of India offer the best healthcare solution to the needy patients because it's the disease for which the drug is manufactured and provided to the end user or patients suffering with ailment. Following examples are provided in the context of 'Many Countries and Many Diseases Strategy (MCMDS)'.

a. Countries like US, Kenya, Brazil, Germany, Tanzania, UK, South Africa, Russia, Nigeria and Australia depend on India for affordable and quality medicines in the therapeutic areas of anti-infectives, cardiovascular, gastrointestinal, vitamins, minerals, respiratory, pain/analgesic and anti-diabetic. That means health services for 80% of the world population rely on Indian pharma. In case of pharmaceutical companies of India, the cost of treating AIDS patients from $50 per day per person to one dollar has dropped down. Life saving medication thus has access by millions of patients. India has provided every fifth generic drug in the world. 'Generic' drugs are chemically the same as brand name drugs, and they are produced once patents expire or no exclusivity exists (Contract-pharma, 2018).

b. Indian pharmaceutical exports were 34% in the financial year 2013/14 accounted by US, followed by Europe (26%) and Asia (20%).

c. Exports to Africa increased at the very substantial compound annual growth rate of 21% from 2009/10 to 2013/14, with antimalarial and antiretroviral HIV/AIDS drugs being the largest components.

d. The world's vaccines about 60% are from India and it exports them to 150 countries.

e. India is one of the greatest success stories in medicine of access to affordable HIV treatment. In the year 1999, World Health Organization (WHO) declared that HIV/AIDS was the No.1 killer in Africa; at that time period, multinational (MNCs) pharmaceutical companies with patent monopolies were charging more than $10,000 per patient per year for antiretroviral (HIV medicines), thereby making treatment economically unviable for millions of patients in the developing world and were solely restricted to a particular class or section of people. India's reputed pharmaceutical company 'Cipla' manufactured and supplied the triple fixed-dose combination of HIV antiretroviral at $1 a day, and since then, this reputed pharmaceutical company has been providing the top notch quality HIV-AIDS-related healthcare solution and providing the relief to a greater extent by taking away all the pain points. Today, world's primary source of affordable HIV medicines comes from India as it is one of the very less countries with the capacity to promptly produce newer HIV generic drugs.

f. The United Nations (UN)'s backed Medicines Patent Pool has signed six different sub-licences with India's most well-known and trusted pharmaceutical companies which are Aurobindo, Desano, Cipla Emcure, Laurus Labs and Hetero Labs which allows them to make generic anti-AIDS medicine named as 'Tenofovir Alafenamide (TAF)' for 112 developing countries around the world.

E. Research & Development and Innovation Strategy (RDIS)

For many decades, pharmaceutical companies of India have made up their mind set as 'Innovate in India and Give to the World', and hence, different pharmaceutical companies of India are spending a huge amount of fund towards R&D activities for coming up with the innovative healthcare solutions which are in urgent need across the globe. India's indigenous and home grown pharmaceutical companies are shifting their business models from low value generics to high value generics which are difficult to copy, and simultaneously, they are inclined to cater to the niche or specialty innovative products including biosimilar drugs.

Following examples are provided pertaining to the R&D and Innovation Strategy (RDIS) practised by different pharmaceutical companies of India.

a. Pharmaceutical companies of India like Lupin, Glenmark, Torrent, Alkem and many more are adopting Research & Development and Innovation Strategy (RDIS) as a route for capturing the generic market is by inventing a new drug delivery system which does not infringe upon the existing process patent of the innovative company and enjoy the benefit of early mover or fast mover advantage with the patent expiry of the product for the familiar drug in different developed and developing nations (Karnani, 2012; Khare, 2014; Nandy, 2020; Pal & Nandy, 2019).

b. Indian research-centric pharmaceutical companies are becoming in the top position as far as the patents in the pharmaceutical sector are concerned. In recent times, more than 45 pharmaceutical companies of India are undergoing various phases of clinical trials for key therapy nearly 135 unique molecules areas such as cancer, allergic rhinitis, diabetes, osteoarthritis, among others. Those molecules are nearly about 30% in phase-3 or clinical trials are in last stage.

c. The innovation in the pharmaceutical industry of India is concentrated mainly on drug combinations (26%), anti-inflammatory drugs (23%), natural products made of plant extracts (19%), antibacterial drugs (17%) and anti-cancer drugs (15%). Indian historical roots and popularity of Ayurveda have concentrated on natural products for pharmaceutical use.

d. The top patent filers in pharmaceutical industry of India include Cadila Healthcare, Dr. Reddy's, Wockhardt, Cipla, Sun Pharma, Aurobindo and Lupin.

e. Top companies on an average have shown an increase in their aggregated R&D expenditure from 6% of sales in 2011 to more than 9% in 2016.

f. As a part of Research & Development and Innovation Strategy (RDIS), a wide spectrum of indications is also covered up, 12 of these 50 active deals are focusing on chronic diseases such as epilepsy, diabetes, dermatology and inflammation, six deals are focusing on developing drugs for antibacterial and antiviral treatments across multiple infections and five deals are focusing on oncology.

g. The in-house R&D effort of pharmaceutical companies of India covers up (I) novel product, (II) advanced process and (III) biopharmaceutical products for enjoying high financial returns and earn about 50–60% of their revenue from the international market like US, Europe, Japan and Australia (Khare, 2014).

h. Dr. Reddy's laboratory and Ranbaxy (currently Sun Pharmaceutical) as early as 1995 the product R&D was first started and today many pharmaceutical companies of India are engaged in product R&D with joint collaboration followed by their core competencies in the manufacturing of drug development to obtain win–win situation (Kiran & Mishra, 2009).

    i. Most of the research-based pharmaceutical companies of India like Sun, Lupin, Cipla, Zydus, Mankind, Intas, Aristro and many more are keeping up the innovation and aggression to stay ahead of competitors like China followed by their low cost of production and the large and strong base of scientific and technical human resources (Kiran & Mishra, 2009; Viswanathan, 2017).

    j. To obtain competitive advantage in the global context, India's research-centric pharmaceutical companies like Sun Pharma total sales on research spent 9.1% and development, Lupin's R&D total sales value spent in budget 12–15% FY 2016 (Kiran & Mishra, 2009).

F. USFDA Business Strategy (USFDA-BS)

Marketing the drug and pharmaceutical products in the US and obtaining required regulatory approval from United States Food and Drug Administration (USFDA) are mandatory, and hence, most of the pharmaceutical companies of India take into account different sorts of preventive and proactive measures to meet the compliance of USFDA and ensure the satisfactory financial returns and constantly engage for enhancing the technical competencies. The accomplishments and attainments which pharmaceutical industry of India has obtained after adopting the USFDA Business Strategy (USFDA-BS) are listed in the following.

    a. India has the 2nd largest number of USFDA-approved manufacturing plants outside the US region. As far as the current statistics are concerned, in India, there are approximately 2,633 FDA-approved drug products. India also has approximately 546 USFDA-approved pharmaceutical companies of India manufacturing sites which is the highest number outside the US Region (Kiran & Mishra, 2009).

    b. India is also the destination of large pool of scientific skills making pharmaceutical companies of India much-sought-after in Contract Research and Manufacturing Services (Kiran & Mishra, 2009).

    c. Pharmaceutical companies of India have obtained 304 Abbreviated New Drug Application approvals from the US Food and Drug Administration in year 2017. The US$70–80 billion US generics market in India accounts for around 30% (by volume) and about 10% (by value) (Kiran & Mishra, 2009).

G. Overseas Production Strategy (OPS)

Apart from export function, some pharmaceutical companies of India set up their manufacturing plants for drug and pharmaceutical product promotion in the land of the foreign countries like Brazil, Mexico and Argentina. The relevant examples are provided in the following.

a. The Glenmark Pharmaceutical Limited is having plant in Buenos Aires and company's global hub has become the manufacture and export of oncological including the US products to over 20 countries (Kiran & Mishra, 2009; Viswanathan, 2017).
b. India's reputed and well-regarded pharmaceutical companies such as Dr. Reddy's Labs, Lupin, Sun Pharmaceuticals and Cipla have also established manufacturing units in the US (Kiran & Mishra, 2009).

H. Biosimilars Business Strategy (BBS)

'Biosimilar Drug' area is very much contemporary in nature and India's biotechnology industry is growing at a satisfactory rate of around 30% a year and will reach US$100 billion by 2025 comprising bio-pharmaceuticals, bio-services, bio-industry and bioinformatics. 'Biosimilar' basically contains vaccines, therapeutics and diagnostics which are extensively used and recommended by the healthcare professionals for the immune-compromising diseases like cancer, HIV-AIDS diabetes, multiple sclerosis, rheumatoid arthritis and psoriasis. For example, Biocon's launch of Herceptin biosimilar (CANMAb) for the treatment of early stage breast cancer is the latest example in this category (Kiran & Mishra, 2009). The biosimilar industry is growing very fast and ensuring many fold growth rate in the forthcoming years, and hence, Indian biotechnological companies are targeting the global biologics market both in domestic and in international context. Pharmaceutical companies of India have various recent investments made outside India which including:

a. Biocon's in Malaysia 200 crore (₹) investment in an insulin plant.

b. Cipla has invested in South Africa 600 crore (₹) investments in biosimilars.

I. Collaborative Business Strategy (CBS)

To obtain the synergistic effects, sometime pharmaceutical companies of India adopt the Collaborative Business Strategy (CBS) to transmit the vision of the organization by utilizing the core competencies of both companies. Pharmaceutical industry of India has two most important forms of collaborative activity noticed in the context:

a. Joint Venture (JV) and
b. Licensing Deal.

In JV schemes, the risk is shared with foreign multinational (MNCs) and pharmaceutical companies of India, whereas in licensing arrangements, an Indian pharmaceutical company licenses out the molecule to foreign MNCs and gets a royalty from the deal (Khare, 2014).

Some of the examples pertaining to the Collaborative Business Strategy (CBS) are:

a. India-based pharmaceutical company Glenmark pharmaceutical has collaborated with US-based pharmaceutical company Merck's generics to capture the Dermatology market of Europe (Khare, 2014).
b. Zydus Cadila, an India-based pharmaceutical company has collaborated with South Australia-based Mayne Pharma to market their anti-cancer product in Australia (Khare, 2014).

Apart from private collaboration, pharmaceutical companies of India are also availing the benefit from reputed research institutes of India like Council of Scientific and Industrial Research, Indian Council of Medical Research and around 30 Indian reputed universities funded by the Ministry of Higher Education, Government of India, for conducting quality R&D activities towards gaining global competitive advantage (Khare, 2014).

REFERENCES

Busru, S. A., & Singh, S. (2017). Bi-directional causality between working capital management and profitability: Empirical study of Indian listed firms. *SSRN Electronic Journal.* https://doi.org/10.2139/ssrn.2928494. Retrieved from https://www.researchgate.net/publication/318000304_Bi-Directional_Causality_between_Working_Capital_Management_and_Profitability_Empirical_Study_of_Indian_Listed_Firms

Contractpharma. (2018). *2018 pharma industry outlook.* Retrieved from https://www.contractpharma.com/issues/2018-01-01/view_features/pharma-industry-outlook/

Gupta, P. (2018). *Trends in pharma export industry in India.* Retrieved from https://www.pharmafocusasia.com/strategy/trends-pharma-export-industry

Karnani, N. (2012). *The pharmaceutical industry project.* Retrieved from https://www.scribd.com/document/86750020/The-Pharmaceutical-Industry-Project

Khare, S. (2014). *An overview of the Indian pharmaceutical sector.* Retrieved from https://www.scribd.com/document/144706191/9783790828757-c2

Kiran, R., & Mishra, S. (2009). Performance of the Indian pharmaceutical industry in post TRIPS period: A firm level analysis. *International Review of Business Research Papers, 5*(6), 148–160. Retrieved from https://www.researchgate.net/publication/258437338_Performance_of_the_Indian_pharmaceutical_industry_in_post-TRIPS_period_a_firm_level_analysis

Nandy, M. (2020). Is there any impact of r&d on financial performance? Evidence from Indian pharmaceutical companies. *FIIB Business Review, 9*(4), 319–334. https://doi.org/10.1177/2319714520981816

Pal, B., & Nandy, M. (2019). Innovation and business sustainability (IBS): Empirical evidence from Indian pharmaceutical industry (IPI). *Artificial Intelligence for Engineering Design, Analysis and Manufacturing., 33*(2), 117–128. https://doi.org/10.1017/S0890060419000040

Sapra, D. (2016). *The world's pill factory.* Retrieved from https://www.dandc.eu/en/article/health-services-80-humanity-depend-drugs-made-india

Viswanathan, R. (2017). *The world is looking for affordable drugs—And India needs to keep delivering.* Retrieved from https://thewire.in/economy/pharmaceutical-drugs-exports-india

CHAPTER 6

Evaluation of Financial Performance in Global Context

6.1 Financial Performance Evaluation: Concept & Meaning

6.1.1 Financial Performance: Meaning & Concept

A particular company's financial performance is solely based on the numbers. It imparts an overview of a company's soundness with respect to financial health of the company. It's also important to understand that financial performance connects to the past, and can't predict the exact image of the future. While evaluating a company's financial performance, it should always be taken into the consideration some crucial factors like comparable business in same sector or segment, overall industry and the company's own historical perspectives. Understanding financial performance is necessary because they help in the decision-making process of the company to take forward the company in a right direction for attaining the business sustainability by maintaining company's financial health (Nandy, 2020; Stobierski, 2020).

The discussion will be made here pertaining to pharmaceutical companies; though the nature of financial principles is same for all types of industries. Since the focus has been made in this book on pharmaceutical sector, the subsequent discussion has been made here pertaining to the pharmaceutical industry. Basically, a pharmaceutical company's financial performance provides the relevant information to the investors about its general business performance. It's a snapshot of its economic health of the company and the responsibilities performed by company's management providing information for the future, whether its operations and profits are on the right track to fuel the growth or not (Nandy, 2020; Pal & Nandy, 2019).

6.1.2   Financial Performance: Key Aspects

The key aspects of financial performance are discussed below:

a. Financial performance provides relevant information to the investors about the general overview of a company. It captures the company's overall financial health and the activities being performed by its management (Nandy, 2020).
b. An important document which records and reports all relevant corporate financial performance sometimes needs to be available in public domain to meet the prescribed regulatory norms and compliance on an annual basis. Most of the pharmaceutical companies listed in the various stock exchanges upload the crucial documents pertaining to the financial performance in their corporate website to make investors or general public aware for financial knowledge dissemination (Nandy, 2020; Pal & Nandy, 2019).
c. Financial statements mainly reviewed in assessing overall financial performance of a pharmaceutical company which includes balance sheet, statement of cash flows and income statement (Nandy, 2020; Pal & Nandy, 2019).
d. The indicators pertaining to financial performance are quantifiable metrics which are applied to measure how well a pharmaceutical company is performing (Nandy, 2020; Pal & Nandy, 2019).
e. Generally, no single measure is recommended to evaluate the financial performance of a pharmaceutical company (Nandy, 2020; Pal & Nandy, 2019).

6.2   OVERVIEW OF 'DUPONT ANALYSIS'

In the next chapter (Chapter 7: Empirical Study), while working with the Dependent Variable: 'Return on Equity' as one of the important financial performance-related measures used in the empirical model conceptualized in the study for evaluating financial performance of sample pharmaceutical companies; the principles of 'DuPont Analysis' have been followed while working with the 'Return on Equity' variable before running the multivariate panel regression model to study the relationship between 'research and development (R&D)' expenditure and 'financial performance' of the Indian pharmaceutical companies. A brief discussion is made below about 'DuPont Analysis' (Wikipedia, 2020).

6.2.1 An Overview

'DuPont Analysis' is also known as 'DuPont Model' or 'DuPont Identity'. It is a framework popularized by the 'DuPont Corporation' for measuring financial performance. The name has derived from 'DuPont Corporation' started using this formula in 1920s. The salesman of 'DuPont Explosives' Donaldson Brown conceptualized this formula and documented it in an internal efficiency official report in 1912, since then 'DuPont Analysis' is a useful technique which is globally accepted to decompose 'different drivers' of 'return on equity' (Wikipedia, 2020).

Decomposition of 'ROE' allows investors eying on the pharmaceutical sector or any other sectors for comparing the operational efficiency of two similar companies operating in the similar industry like pharmaceutical industry. Professionals working in pharmaceutical companies may study this analysis to evaluate strengths or weaknesses of company; these are addressed to determine what financial activities are contributing the most for the changes observed in 'ROE' (Wikipedia, 2020).

6.2.2 Features of 'DuPont Analysis'

The key features of DuPont Analysis are listed below:

a. This analysis is generally adopted to evaluate the important parts of a company's 'ROE'.
b. There are basically three important financial metrics that drive 'ROE', which are listed below

    i. Operating efficiency: It is measured by 'net income' divided by 'total sales' or 'revenue'.
    ii. Asset use efficiency: It is measured by the asset turnover ratio.

iii. Financial leverage: It is measured by the 'equity multiplier', which is equal to 'average assets' divided by 'average equity'.

c. The 'DuPont Analysis' is basically a framework which was popularized by the 'DuPont Corporation' in global context for interpreting basic financial performance by taking into consideration of 'ROE' (Wikipedia, 2020).

d. It's a useful technique which is generally applied to decompose the different drivers of 'ROE' (Wikipedia, 2020).

6.2.3   *'DuPont Analysis' vs. 'ROE'*

ROE metric is measured with respect to net income divided by shareholders' equity. The 'DuPont Analysis' is an expanded version of 'ROE'. The 'ROE' calculation itself reveals how well a company utilizes capital from shareholders (Wikipedia, 2020). With this analysis, investors and analysts can further narrow down what drives make a significant change in 'ROE' or why the 'ROE' is considered to be high or low? Therefore, this strategic analysis can help to provide right signal pertaining to its profitability and tries to point out the main cause of satisfactory 'ROE' by asking some questions like: because of assets utilization in an appropriate manner there is a positive impact on ROE, or owing to debt that is driving 'ROE'? (Wikipedia, 2020).

6.3   Widely Adopted Financial Performance Metrics in the Pharmaceutical Industry

Worldwide financial performance metrics and measures which are generally adopted to understand are discussed below. Financial performance indicators are also known as 'key performance indicators (KPIs)', which are quantifiable measurements and used to decide, track and project the economic well-being of a pharmaceutical business or any other business (Stobierski, 2020). These financial metrics act as scientific tools and techniques for both corporate insiders (like management and board members) and outsiders (like research analysts and investors) to understand how well a company is performing specifically with regard to its competitors in the similar sector and identify where the strengths and weaknesses lie (Stobierski, 2020). The most internationally used financial performance indicators in pharmaceutical sector and other sectors are listed below.

SI No	Financial performance metric	Explanation
1	Gross profit /gross profit margin	The amount of revenue made from sales after subtracting production costs, and the percentage amount a company earns per dollar ($) of sales (Stobierski, 2020)
2	Net profit/net profit margin	The amount of revenue from sales after subtracting all related business expenses and taxes, and the related ratio of earnings per dollar ($) of sales (Stobierski, 2020)
3	Working capital	Immediately available or highly liquid funds, used to finance day-to-day business operations (Stobierski, 2020)
4	Operating cash flow	The amount of money being generated by regular business operations (Stobierski, 2020)
5	Current ratio	'A measure of solvency': total assets divided by total liabilities (Stobierski, 2020)
6	Debt-to-equity ratio	A company's total liabilities divided by its shareholder equity (Nandy, 2020; Stobierski, 2020)
7	Quick ratio	Another solvency measure, which calculates the percentage of very liquid current assets (cash, securities, accounts receivables) against total liabilities (Stobierski, 2020)
8	Inventory turnover	How much inventory is sold within a certain period, and how often the entire inventory was sold (Stobierski, 2020)?
9	Return on equity	Net income divided by shareholder equity (a company's assets minus its debts) (Nandy, 2020; Pal & Nandy, 2019; Stobierski, 2020)
10	Return on assets	Return on assets, or ROA, is another profitability ratio, similar to ROE, which is measured by dividing net profit by the company's average assets. It's an indicator which explains how well a company is managing its available resources and assets to net higher profits (Nandy, 2020; Pal & Nandy, 2019; Stobierski, 2020)

(continued)

(continued)

SI No	Financial performance metric	Explanation
11	Sales turnover	Sales turnover is the company's total amount of products or services sold over a given period of time—typically in an accounting year (Nandy, 2020; Pal & Nandy, 2019; Stobierski, 2020)
12	Market capitalization	Market Capitalization, commonly called market cap, is the market value of a publicly traded company's outstanding shares. Market Capitalization is equal to the share price multiplied by the number of shares outstanding (Nandy, 2020; Pal & Nandy, 2019)

Financial analysis is extremely essential for every organization to understand its present financial position and analyse its future financial goals. It is an indicator to decide if the company is going on the right track or not; judicious decision is also taken if there are any changes required in the business function. Financial performance will be positive if all things and strategies are functioning well in organization, and it would be negative if things are not working in favour of the company as per the business objective set. In the next chapter, discussion is further made with regard to different financial performance measures.

REFERENCES

Nandy, M. (2020). Is there any impact of r&d on financial performance? Evidence from Indian pharmaceutical companies. *FIIB Business Review, 9*(4), 319–334. https://doi.org/10.1177/2319714520981816

Pal, B., & Nandy, M. (2019). Innovation and business sustainability (IBS): Empirical evidence from Indian pharmaceutical industry (IPI). *Artificial Intelligence for Engineering Design, Analysis and Manufacturing, 33*(2), 117–128. https://doi.org/10.1017/S0890060419000040

Stobierski, T. (2020). *13 financial performance measures managers should monitor*. Retrieved from https://online.hbs.edu/blog/post/financial-performance-measures

Wikipedia. (2020). *DuPont analysis*. Retrieved from https://en.wikipedia.org/wiki/DuPont_analysis

CHAPTER 7

Empirical Study

7.1 Objectives and Hypotheses of the Study

In this section, an attempt has been made to study the relationship between R&D activities undertaken by the NSE-listed Indian pharmaceutical companies and financial performance. In this study, financial performance is being measured by Return on Assets (ROA), Return on Equity (ROE), Sales Turnover and Market Capitalization (Nandy, 2020; Pal & Nandy, 2019). In the light of this context, four hypotheses have been formulated as listed below to satisfy the objective of the study.

Hypothesis I: R&D activities and Sales Turnover

H_1: *R&D activities have relation with Sales Turnover.*

Hypothesis II: R&D activities and Return on Assets

H_2: *R&D activities have relation with Return on Assets.*

Hypothesis III: R&D activities and Return on Equity

H_3: *R&D activities have relation with Return on Equity.*

Hypothesis IV: R&D activities and Market Capitalization.

H_4: *R&D activities have relation with Market Capitalization.*

M. Nandy, *Relationship between R&D and Financial Performance in Indian Pharmaceutical Industry,* https://doi.org/10.1007/978-981-16-6921-7_7

7.2   RESEARCH METHODOLOGY

Complete step-wise procedures have been performed in this study discussed below in a systematic manner (Nandy, 2020; Pal & Nandy, 2019).

7.2.1   Data Collection

This study has been carried out with the help of secondary data. The data pertaining to Sales Turnover, Market Capitalization, R&D Expenses, Advertisement and Marketing Expenses, Capital Intensity, Leverage Ratio and Operating Expenditure to Total Assets Ratio pertaining to NSE-listed Indian pharmaceutical companies has been collected from the following sources (Nandy, 2020; Pal & Nandy, 2019).

Data Sources:

 a. Capital Market Publishers India Ltd.
 b. Sample Companies' Annual Reports.
 c. Press Releases.
 d. *ORG-IMS* Research Private Limited.
 e. Corporate Brochure of Pharmaceutical Companies and
 f. *AIOCD* Pharmasofttech AWACS Pvt. Ltd.

7.2.2   Sampling Technique and Sample Size

A total pharmaceutical company involved in Indian pharmaceutical market space has been considered as 'population size' in this study. After an in-depth analysis of the annual reports of different pharmaceutical companies, 63 pharmaceutical companies have been incurring R&D expenditure regularly during the study period, and hence, these 63 pharmaceutical companies for this study have been considered based on the 'Stratified Sampling Technique' (Nandy, 2020; Pal & Nandy, 2019). To define the entire population of pharmaceutical companies operating in pharmaceutical industry of India space and to obtain a complete insight of the impact of R&D activities on financial performance, there are two categories of pharmaceutical sample companies chosen in this study. A specific code has been assigned to a specific category of pharmaceutical

Table 7.1 Codes of sample companies

Company category type/code	Company type description	Turnover (₹)	No. of sample companies	Measurement unit of sales turnover
A	Comprised of subsidiaries of Multinational Companies (MNCs)	Annual sales turnover irrespective of any	26	Indian Rupee (₹)
B	Comprised of large-scale Indian pharmaceutical companies	Annual sale turnover of more than (>) Rs 300 Crores	37	Indian Rupee (₹)

Note Total Number of Sample Companies Considered for the Study = 63
Source Author's own

company type and for the convenience of the interpretation of all and the same will be used in the upcoming sections of the study.

From Table 7.1, we can find the different types of NSE-listed Indian pharmaceutical companies as sample companies which will help us to evaluate the impact of R&D activities on their financial performance.

7.2.3   Study Period

The study period from 1995 to 2015 has been selected for the following reasons.

a. R&D work orientation began in the pharmaceutical industry of India from the year 1990 onwards. But the appropriate data was available from 1995 since 1990–1994 was the gestation period and during this time no required data had been found for this study (Nandy, 2020; Pal & Nandy, 2019).
b. For performing pharmaceutical R&D activities, long time is required. For example, to develop a New Molecular Entity, New Chemical Entity or Novel Drug Delivery Systems as part of R&D Activities, most of the time it takes approximately 15 to 20 years (Nandy, 2020; Pal & Nandy, 2019).
c. In 2005, India introduced the product patent regime in the country and

d. 'The Patents (Amendment) Act, 2005' is the third of three amendments to the 'Patents Act of 1970', to bring India's patent regime into compliance with the 'WTO (World Trade Organization) TRIPS (Trade Related Intellectual Property Rights) Agreement' (Nandy, 2020; Pal & Nandy, 2019). With this amendment, Indian pharmaceutical companies started investing adequate amount of fund for performing different R&D activities (Nandy, 2020; Pal & Nandy, 2019).

7.2.4   *Tools & Techniques*

Descriptive statistics and inferential techniques have been used in this study for analytical purpose. To examine the relationship between R&D activities and financial performance, panel regression analysis with the help of STATA Software (version 12) has been performed.

7.3   Conceptual Model for the Study

The concept of business sustainability is managing the triple dimension which mainly is a process by which companies effectively manage their financial, environmental and social risks. It also takes into account different opportunities and obligations. These impacts are referred to as '3 Ps' denoted as profits, people and planet. Ram Nidumolu (2009) in his interview published in the 'The New Work Times' blog has defined business sustainability as 'A mind-set of sustainability = innovation' which is essential for making a real evolution to the global economy. It's imperative to mention that in emerging economies like India providing right medicine at the right time and at the right place with an affordable cost is really challenging task for the Indian pharmaceutical companies (Pal & Nandy, 2019). However, these challenges are being managed by the pharmaceutical companies of India by being proactive and not being reactive and hence Indian pharmaceutical companies have been constantly taking endeavour for providing innovative and satisfactory healthcare solutions by conducting different R&D with an affordable cost to the needy patients' fraternities (Pal & Nandy, 2019). India is having a large number of scientists who are continuously taking painstaking efforts to discover the novel drug discovery and constantly cultivating their minds for drug discoveries and innovation (Pal & Nandy, 2019). Indian pharmaceutical companies are getting New Chemical Entities, successfully filing bulk number of patents and enjoying Intellectual Property Rights and getting approvals from the USFDA for different drug discoveries and innovation (Pal & Nandy, 2019). We can also find that a large number of developed nations (US, UK) are highly dependent on pharmaceutical companies of India. Because of the past experience in last few decades, these developed nations have developed the faith on the quality pharmaceutical products innovated by the pharmaceutical companies of India (Pal & Nandy, 2019). At present, greater than 80 per cent of antiretroviral drugs consumed globally to combat AIDS (Acquired Immune Deficiency Syndrome) are provided by the pharmaceutical companies of India. These R&D activities are constantly helping Indian pharmaceutical companies to enjoy business sustainability (Pal & Nandy, 2019). Innovation plays a crucial role and acts as a strategic tool for fuelling the growth and defining the success of Indian pharmaceutical business, and finally helps the organizations to adapt and grow in the marketplace (Pal & Nandy, 2019). Being innovative does not only mean inventing, in broader perspectives innovation can mean adapting to changes in the business environment to deliver novel drug products or healthcare services to face any unprecedented healthcare challenges and crisis (Pal & Nandy, 2019). The successful exploitation of innovative ideas is crucial to a business function which enables to improve its processes, bring new and improved products and services to market, increase its efficiency and, most importantly, improve its profitability. The profitability can also be in the form of Sales Turnover, Return on Assets, Return on Equity or Market Capitalization (Pal & Nandy, 2019).

In Emerging economies like India are finding rapid growth of chronic 'Western' diseases like 'chronic respiratory problems', 'diabetes, hypertension', 'cancer', 'heart disease' and 'neurological disorders'. Some specific disease like 'diabetes' are gradually becoming into near-epidemic situation (Pal & Nandy, 2019). In India, for example, the occurrence of 'diabetes' and 'cancer' is anticipated to rise in many folds in the years to come (Pal & Nandy, 2019). In the current scenario, innovation is the need of the hour in India's pharmaceutical industry. The current population of India is approximately 1.3 billion and is having the large patient pool, constantly escalating the cost of treatments and increasing risk factors of 'chronic diseases' due to lifestyle change. The Government of India and the pharmaceutical Industry of India are constantly collaborating together, exchanging dialogues and providing focus to boost innovation and discoveries in the India's pharmaceutical sector (Pal &

Nandy, 2019). Many initiatives are constantly taken by the GoI to boost innovation and protect 'intellectual property rights'. Moreover, in pharmaceutical industry, R&D activities are undertaken for the innovation and research purpose (Pal & Nandy, 2019). It is essential to market innovative healthcare solution for the benefit of society at large, and hence, Indian pharmaceutical companies are conducting R&D activities for novel drug discoveries and ensuring satisfactory financial returns (Pal & Nandy, 2019). The financial performance can be in the form of:

- Sales Turnover
- Return on Assets (ROA)
- Return on Equity (ROE) and
- Market Capitalization

The framework pertaining to theoretical foundation of the study is shown in the following Fig. 7.1.

The RDFP Framework has been conceptualized for this study based on the hypotheses postulated for establishing the relationship between R&D activities and financial performance.

7.4   Description of Variables Incorporated in the Study

For performing the empirical analysis, various dependent variables (DV), independent variables (IV) and control variables (CV) have been incorporated for the need of the empirical study for measuring the impact of R&D activities of listed Indian pharmaceutical companies on their financial performance. In the following, a detailed discussion is made of all the dependent variables (DV), independent variables (IV) and control variables which have been used for this study (Nandy, 2020; Pal & Nandy, 2019).

7.5   Definition, Description, Measurement and Proposed Hypotheses with Respect to Dependent Variables (DV)

After going through the existing literatures, we come to know various measures of financial performance. In this study, the financial performance-related variables which have considered are solely based on

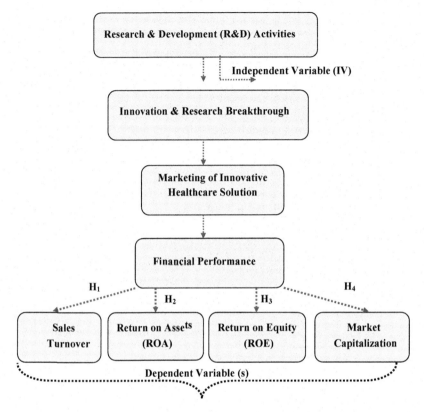

Fig. 7.1 Research & Development and Financial Performance Framework [RDFP Framework] (*Source* Conceptualized by the author)

the relevance of the study and contemporary approach of measuring. For conducting the panel regression analysis, consideration has been made for four (4) financial performance-related Dependent Variables (DV) which are Sales Turnover (ST), Return on Assets (ROA), Return on Equity (ROE) and Market Capitalization (MC), and a brief discussion of these variables is given in the following.

I. *Sales Turnover*

Sales turnover is the total amount of revenue generated by the pharmaceutical companies during the study period 1995–2015.

The data has been captured for the period of April to March for every financial year for the period of 1995–2015. The concept of sales turnover is useful for tracking sales levels on a trend line through multiple measurement periods (yearly basis) in order to spot meaningful changes in the selling activity level of a particular pharmaceutical company (Nandy, 2020; Pal & Nandy, 2019). Financial performance is powerfully impacted by sales turnover, which in turn is strongly dependent on R&D Intensity (Nandy, 2020; Pal & Nandy, 2019). The authors also highlighted the positive impact of R&D activity on sales turnover. In this study, natural logarithm of sales turnover (variable name used as LN_ST) has used. The reason for which logarithm of sales turnover has been incorporated in this study is to ensure measurement compatibility with the other variables used in the panel regression model (Pal & Nandy, 2019). The calculation period of sales turnover is one financial year (1 April to 31 March).

Mathematical Expression:

$$\text{Sales Turnover} = \text{Monthly Sales} \times 12\,\text{Months}.$$

With respect to this study, following hypothesis will be tested.

H_1: *R&D activities have significant relation with Sales Turnover.*

II. **Return on Assets (ROA)**

ROA is an indicator which measures how efficient the management is in converting the assets of the firms into net income. ROA is calculated by dividing a company's annual earnings by its total assets (Nandy, 2020; Pal & Nandy, 2019; Tyagi, & Nauriyal, 2016).

Mathematical Expression:

$$\text{ROA} = \frac{\text{Annual Earnings}}{\text{Total Assets}}$$

With respect to this study following hypothesis, we would like to test.

H_2: *R&D activities have relation with Return on Assets.*

III. *Return on Equity (ROE)*
ROE is a significant indicator that shows how well the owners' resources have been utilized by the firm to achieve the most desirable objective of shareholders' wealth maximization. ROE is generally net income divided by equity (Nandy, 2020; Pal & Nandy, 2019; Tyagi, & Nauriyal, 2016). In this study, ROE has been used as percentage (%).
Mathematical Expression:

$$ROE = \frac{Net\,Income}{Equity}$$

To satisfy the research objective, following hypothesis will be tested.

H₃: *R&D activities have relation with Return on Equity.*

IV. *Market Capitalization*
Market Capitalization is the amount of monetary resources it would require to purchase an entire company based on its current stock price (Nandy, 2020; Pal & Nandy, 2019). It is calculated by multiplying the total number of shares outstanding by the current price of a single share of stock (Nandy, 2020; Pal & Nandy, 2019; Tyagi, & Nauriyal, 2016).
Mathematical Expression:

$$Market\,Capitalization = Total\,Number\,of\,Shares\,Outstanding$$
$$\times\,Present\,Share\,Price$$

In this study, Natural Logarithm of Market Capitalization (variable used as Ln_MC) has been applied to ensure measurement compatibility with the other variables.
With respect to this research work, following hypothesis will be tested as well.

H₄: *R&D activities have relation with Market Capitalization.*

In this study, financial performance of pharmaceutical companies of different categories has been measured in terms of profitability rather than in terms of 'innovative outputs' such as productivity or number of patents filed (Nandy, 2020; Pal & Nandy, 2019).

7.6   DEFINITION, DESCRIPTION
AND MEASUREMENT OF INDEPENDENT VARIABLE (IV)

Research and Development Intensity (RDI) as independent variable has been used for this study for measuring the impact of R&D activities of different listed Indian pharmaceutical companies on their financial performance, and with the respect to the research and development, required hypotheses have been postulated for this study. A short discussion of RDI is made in the following.

I. *Research and Development Intensity (RDI)*

Existing literatures indicate that R&D expenditure of a pharmaceutical company impacts its profitability positively (Nandy, 2020; Pal & Nandy, 2019; Tyagi, & Nauriyal, 2016). The explanation to this postulation lies pertaining to the fact that different kinds of R&D activities enable the Indian pharmaceutical companies to generate satisfactory financial returns which in turn may support further R&D expenditure and keep the pharmaceutical companies in the forefront as well as enable the pharmaceutical companies to gain the competitive advantage by marketing the innovative healthcare solution for taking care of the different unmet healthcare need to treat the novel diseases and disorders (Nandy, 2020; Pal & Nandy, 2019; Tyagi, & Nauriyal, 2016). In this study, Independent Variable, Research and Development Intensity (RDI) is considered as pharmaceutical company's R&D expenditures to its same year's net sales for ensuring the robustness of panel regression (Nandy, 2020; Pal & Nandy, 2019).

Mathematical Expression:

$$\text{Research \& Development Intensity} = \frac{\text{Research \& Development Expenditure}}{\text{Net Sales}}$$

7.7   CONTROL VARIABLE (CV) DESCRIPTION

The study of existing literature suggests that there are several other variables that may also affect the financial performance of pharmaceutical companies in addition to the effect of R&D, and therefore, it becomes pertinent to include these Control Variables while analysing the impact of R&D activities of NSE-listed Indian pharmaceutical companies on their financial performance. In this study, Control Variables (CV) have been incorporated in the panel regression models in order to assess the relationship between the Independent Variable (IV) and Dependent Variable (DV). These Control Variables (CV) might impact the relationship between R&D expenditure and financial performance of pharmaceutical companies operating in Indian space (Nandy, 2020; Pal & Nandy, 2019).

I. *Advertising and Marketing Intensity (AMI)*
Advertising and marketing activities increase the brand recognition and brand recall. It also ensures recognition for the pharmaceutical companies to get hold of a higher price of the products relative to products of its competitors that may be similar in terms of physical appearance and features in a specific market place (Nandy, 2020; Pal & Nandy, 2019; Tyagi, & Nauriyal, 2016). In this study, Advertisement and Marketing Intensity (AMI) is calculated based on Advertising and Marketing Expenditure as percentage of net sales in the given year.
Mathematical Expression:

$$\text{Advertisement\&Marketing Intensity} = \frac{\text{Advertisement\&Marketing Expenditure}}{\text{Net Sales}}$$

II. *Capital Intensity (CI)*
Pharmaceutical industry is a capital intensive industry since adequate amount of capital is highly required to sustain in the pharmaceutical market space (Nandy, 2020; Pal & Nandy, 2019; Tyagi, & Nauriyal, 2016). Thus, in this study, fixed assets as percentage (%) of net sales in the given year have been considered.
Mathematical Expression:

$$\text{Capital Intensity} = \frac{\text{Fixed Assets}}{\text{Net Sales}}$$

III. *Leverage Ratio (LR)*
In the context of pharmaceutical industry, the meaning of Leverage Ratio plays a significant role. As far as the definition goes, Leverage Ratio (LR) is one of the financial measures that try to capture the light with respect to how much capital flow comes in the pharmaceutical business operation in the form of debt (loans) or assesses the ability of a pharmaceutical company to meet its financial obligations (Nandy, 2020; Pal & Nandy, 2019; Tyagi, & Nauriyal,

2016). Thus, in order to capture the effect of leverage on the financial performance of the Indian pharmaceutical companies, total debt as a percentage (%) of total assets (equity), in the given year, has been incorporated in this study. Following mathematical expression has been used to measure the Leverage Ratio for this study.

Mathematical Expression:

$$\text{Leverage Ratio} = \frac{\text{Debt}}{\text{Equity}}$$

IV. *Operating Expenditure to the Total Assets Ratio (OER)*

In pharmaceutical industry, an operating expenditure is a recurring cost for managing the business system seamlessly. Operating expenses to total assets ratio is a measure of managing operational efficiency of a pharmaceutical company which explains the quality and soundness of the business organization or management (Nandy, 2020; Pal & Nandy, 2019; Tyagi, & Nauriyal, 2016). 'Operating expenses to total assets ratio' (OER) has been incorporated in the study as Control Variable to explore the relationship between operational efficiency and financial performance of Indian pharmaceutical companies (Nandy, 2020; Pal & Nandy, 2019) listed with the national stock exchange of India. The following mathematical expression has been used to measure the Operating Expenditure to Total Assets Ratio in this study.

Mathematical Expression:

$$\text{Operating Expenditure to Total Assets Ratio} = \frac{\text{Operating Expenditure}}{\text{Total Assets}}$$

7.8   Overall Description of Variables (DV, CV and IV)

The complete descriptions of all the variables pertaining to the following types of variables have been incorporated in this empirical study as shown in the following Table 7.2.

Table 7.2 Description of overall variables used in the panel regression models

Variable code	Variable description	Variable notation	Variable type	Mathematical expression
Y1	Sales Turnover	ST	Dependent	Ln_ST
Y2	Return on Assets	ROA	(DV)	Annual
Y3	Return on Equity	ROE	Dependent (DV)	Earnings/Total
Y4	Market Capitalization	MC	Dependent (DV) Dependent (DV)	Assets Net Income/Equity Ln_MC
X1	Research & Development Intensity	RDI	Independent (IV)	Research & Development Expenditure/Total Sales
X2	Advertising & Marketing Intensity	AMI	Control (CV)	Advertising & Marketing Expenditure/Total Sales
X3	Capital Intensity	CI	Control (CV)	Fixed Assets/Total Sales
X4	Leverage Ratio	LR	Control (CV)	Debt/Equity
X5	Business Expenses to Total Assets Ratio	OER	Control (CV)	Operating Expenditure/Total Assets

Source Author's own

a. Dependent Variable (DV)
b. Independent Variable (IV)
c. Control Variable (CV)

Table 7.2 basically gives the overall view of various kinds of variables (DV, IV and CV) that are needed in the panel regression model for developing the relationship between financial performance and R&D activities.

7.9 Specification of Different Category Companies Codes for Running Panel Regression Models

To define the entire population pertain to pharmaceutical companies operating in the pharmaceutical industry of India and to obtain a complete insight of the impact of R&D activities on financial performance of the Indian pharmaceutical companies listed with the national

Table 7.3   Codes of sample companies for running panel regression models

Company category/type code	Company type description	Turnover (₹)	No. of sample companies	Measurement unit of sales turnover
A	Comprised of subsidiaries of Multi National Companies (MNCs)	Annual sales turnover irrespective of any	26	Indian Rupee (₹)
B	Comprised of large-scale Indian pharmaceutical companies	Annual sale turnover of more than (>) Rs 300 Crores	37	Indian Rupee (₹)

Source Author's own

stock exchange (NSE) of India, there are four categories of pharmaceutical sample companies chosen and used in this study. A specific code has been allotted to a specific category of pharmaceutical company type, and for the convenience of the interpretation, all these codes pertaining to the respective category of pharmaceutical companies will be used in the upcoming sections of the study (Nandy, 2020; Pal & Nandy, 2019).

From Table 7.3, we can visualize the different types of pharmaceutical companies which will help to run the panel regression models as well as to establish the relationship between R&D activities and financial performance.

7.10   Empirical Model Specification

In this study, to determine the significant impact of R&D activities of various types of pharmaceutical companies on their financial performance, panel regression model has been implicated in the study with the help of strongly balanced panel dataset by inducing four different financial performance-related variables: Sales Turnover (Ln_ST), Return on Assets (ROA), Return on Equity (ROE) and Market Capitalization (Ln_MC) simultaneously (Nandy, 2020; Pal & Nandy, 2019). For each category pharmaceutical companies (category: A and B), following empirical models have been estimated in this study:

$$\text{Ln\_ST}_{it} = \alpha + \beta_{1it}\text{RDI}_{it} + \beta_2\text{AMI}_{it} + \beta_3\text{CI}_{it}$$
$$+ \beta_4\text{LR}_{it} + \beta_5\text{OER}_{it} + \text{\euro}_{it} \tag{7.1}$$

$$\text{ROA}_{it} = \alpha + \beta_1\text{RDI}_{it} + \beta_2\text{AMI}_{it} + \beta_3\text{CI}_{it}$$
$$+ \beta_4\text{LR}_{it} + \beta_5\text{OER}_{it} + \text{\euro}_{it} \tag{7.2}$$

$$\text{ROE}_{it} = \alpha + \beta_1\text{RDI}_{it} + \beta_2\text{AMI}_{it} + \beta_3\text{CI}_{it}$$
$$+ \beta_4\text{LR}_{it} + \beta_5\text{OER}_{it} + \text{\euro}_{it} \tag{7.3}$$

$$\text{Ln\_MC}_{it} = \alpha + \beta_1\text{RDI}_{it} + \beta_2\text{AMI}_{it} + \beta_3\text{CI}_{it}$$
$$+ \beta_4\text{LR}_{it} + \beta_5\text{OER}_{it} + \text{\euro}_{it} \tag{7.4}$$

where,

Ln_ST_{it} = Natural Logarithm of Sales Turnover
ROA_{it} = Return on Assets
ROE_{it} = Return on Equity
Ln_MC_{it} = Natural Logarithm of Market Capitalization
RDI_{it} = Research & Development Intensity
AMI_{it} = Advertisement & Marketing Intensity
CI_{it} = Capital Intensity
LR_{it} = Leverage Ratio
OER_{it} = Operating Expenditure to Total Assets Ratio
$\text{\euro}_{it}$ = Error Term

To complete this empirical study pertain to all category pharmaceutical companies (category: A and B), certain steps have been followed in a chronological order and a brief description of the same is given in the following.

Step 1: Arrangement of Strongly Balanced Panel Dataset
After collecting cross-sectional and time series data from the sample, strongly balanced panel dataset has been arranged for the analysis of this empirical study.

Step 2: Studies of Descriptive Statistics
After the arrangement of the strongly balanced panel dataset, the study of descriptive statistics has been performed by incorporating all Dependent (DV), Independent (IV) and Control (CV) Variables incorporated in the study. In this study, descriptive statistics has been studied to know the nature of sample properly.

Step 3: Studies of Bivariate Correlation Matrix
The study of Bivariate Correlation Matrix has been performed to know the relationship between the two variables and this matrix will also help us to know the strength of relationship between the two variables used in this empirical study.

Step 4: Conduction of Diagnostic Tests
In this study, two specific diagnostic tests have been performed and a brief discussion is made in the following for these two (2) diagnostic tests.

a. *Variation Inflation Factor (VIF)*
   Variation Inflation Factor (VIF) as an econometric test has been performed before running all the panel regression models. With the help of this econometric test, we will be able to know that balanced set of data which will be used in this context is undoubtedly in not having multicollinearity, and the test is for all Explanatory Variables incorporated in this study.

b. *Skewness/Kurtosis Tests*
   Skewness/Kurtosis Tests (SK Test) have been performed in this empirical study for checking the normality of all empirical models to be estimated in the panel regression models. With the help of this diagnostic test, we will come to know that the sample dataset to be used in all empirical models is normally distributed.

Step 5: Estimation of Panel Regression Analysis
In the next stage, we will find the regression analysis by incorporating the Dependent Variables: Sales Turnover (Ln_ST), Return on Assets (ROA), Return on Equity (ROE) and Market Capitalization (Ln_MC) one by one. We will also find that two models related to Panel Data Analysis have been estimated and the models are given below:

a. Fixed Effect Model (FEM) and
b. Random Effect Model (REM).

Step 6: Appropriate Model Selection through Hausman Test
In this step, Hausman Specification Test (popularly known as Hausman Test) has been applied for picking up the correct model of panel regression analysis between Fixed Effect Model and Random Effect Model, and the study of the appropriate model as per the Hausman Test has been discussed in this study.

Step 7: Summarized Results of Four (4) Empirical Models
In this section, based on the appropriate model selection as per Hausman Test, the summarized results of four (4) empirical models have been displayed for all different category companies. This study is consisting with two (2) different category pharmaceutical companies. For each category pharmaceutical companies, four (4) panel regression models have been estimated by incorporating four (4) different Dependent Variables: Sales Turnover (Ln_ST), Return on Assets (ROA), Return on Equity (ROE) and Market Capitalization (Ln_MC) one after another, and hence, total number of empirical models associated with this study are eight (2 Category Pharmaceutical Companies × 4 Empirical Models = 8 Empirical Models). Now, an attempt has been taken to move forward for category-wise (A and B) empirical study by following Step-1 to Step-7 as mentioned in the previous section.

7.11   EMPIRICAL STUDY OF COMPANY CATEGORY: A

First of all, an attempt has been taken to measure the impact of R&D activities pertain to Company Category: A consisting with pharmaceutical companies of different multinational (MNC) subsidiary companies having operation in India irrespective of any sales turnover.

From Table 7.4, we come to know the list of Category-A companies taken for the empirical study. In the following, the empirical study pertaining to Category-A companies is discussed.

7.11.1   Descriptive Statistics

In this part, the basic statistical values of the variables have been dealt with which are calculated. In this study, descriptive statistics has been applied for explaining the primary features of the data, by analysing descriptive statistics to brief the sample and the measures.

Table 7.5 shows the complete analysis of 546 observations which is the product of 26 MNC subsidiaries companies working in India for the duration of 21 years (from 1995 to 2015). The mean of Research and Development Expenditure (Independent Variable: RDI) deployed by the sample pharmaceutical companies is 0.76 crore. There are varieties in case of R&D Expenditure where the minimum amount is 0.22 crore and

Table 7.4 List of Category-A companies

Sl. no	Company name	Sl. no	Company name
1	Pharmacia Healthcare Private Limited	16	GE Healthcare Worldwide
2	Astrazeneca Pharma India Limited	17	Solvay Pharma India Limited
3	Boehringer Ingelheim	18	Fres.Kabi Oncology Limited
4	Abbott India Limited	19	Merck Specialities Private Limited
5	Burroughs Wel -M	20	Makson Pharmaceuticals (I) Pvt. Limited
6	Wyeth Pharmaceuticals Limited	21	Sandoz Pvt. Ltd
7	Roche Limited	22	Holden Medical Laboratories Pvt. Ltd
8	Smith. B. P (Mer)	23	Allergan India Private Limited
9	Fulford (India) Limited	24	Abbott Healthcare Private Limited
10	Glaxo Smith Kline Pharmaceuticals Limited	25	Reckitt Benckiser Healthcare India Pvt. Ltd
11	Novartis India Limited	26	Claris Injectables Limited
12	Sanofi India Limited		
13	Organon (India) Pvt. Ltd		
14	Parke Davis (India) Limited		
15	Pfizer Limited		

Source Author's own

maximum amount is 1.39 crore. This dispersion is also supported by standard deviation of 0.29 crore. It is noticed that the sample companies are incurring 2.37 times less in the areas of Advertising and Marketing Expenditure (Control Variable: AMI) in comparison with R&D Expenditure since the average Advertising and Marketing Expenditure is 0.32 crore. In case of AMI, the values are spread with minimum of 0.22 crore and maximum of 0.55 crore where the standard deviation is 0.07 crore. The average amount of Capital Intensity employed by the sample companies is 0.31 crore. The values of CI is also dispersed where the minimum is 0.06 crore and maximum is 5.22 crore, and this dispersion is well supported by standard deviation 0.72 crore. The sample pharmaceutical companies are using Leverage Ratio where the ratio is 56.94% whose minimum value is 0.26 and maximum value is 1.07. In case of LR, the dispersion is supported by standard deviation 0.22. The sample pharmaceutical

Table 7.5 Descriptive statistics of Category-A companies

Variable	Obs	Mean	Std. dev	Min	Max
LN_ST (₹ Cr.)	546	7.965073	2.965053	0	14.48
ROA (%)	546	0.500293	0.3946415	0	1.29
ROE (%)	546	0.7628938	0.2940624	0.2	1.39
LN_MC (₹ Cr.)	546	8.679304	2.851916	0.72	17.6
RDI (%)	546	0.7630769	0.293369	0.22	1.39
AMI (%)	546	0.325641	0.0790775	0.22	0.55
CI (%)	546	0.315348	0.7292421	0.06	5.22
LR (%)	546	0.5694689	0.2279818	0.26	1.07
OER (%)	546	0.3530586	0.6253334	0.01	5.79

Source Author's own calculation in Stata Software (version 12)

companies have employed operating cost (Control Variable: OER) with an average cost amount 0.35 crore, and these costs are widely spread where the minimum cost is 0.01 crore and maximum cost is 5.79 crore. The spread of this OER cost is supported by the standard deviation of 0.52 crore. Average Sales Turnover (Dependent Variable: Ln_ST) clocked by the sample pharmaceutical companies is 7.96 crore. The Return on Assets (Dependent Variable: ROA) is 50% for the study period where the Return on Equity (Dependent Variable: ROE) is 76.28%. The sample pharmaceutical companies have an average Market Capitalization (Dependent Variable: Ln_MC) of 8.67 crore. This Market Capitalization of sample companies is much spread where minimum Market Capitalization is 0.72 crore and the maximum Market Capitalization is 17.6 crore. This dispersion is supported by standard deviation of 2.85.

7.11.2   Bivariate Correlation Matrix

The Bivariate Correlation Matrix is an analysis of the relationship between the matrix of two variables and a binary relationship that helps us to know if there is a partial relationship in any included dataset. Prior to conducting our panel regression analysis, the bipolar correlation matrix was included as an econometric test to confirm that there was no serial relationship (>0.80) in our well-balanced panel dataset.

From the Bivariate Correlation Matrix presented in Table 7.6, we can find the bivariate correlation between Dependent Variable verses Independent Variable and Control Variables. Matrix Dependent Variables (DV) are LNPP, ROA, ROE and LN_MC, RDI is an Independent Variable (IV)

Table 7.6 Bivariate correlation matrix of Category-A companies

Variables	LN_ST Coefficient (p value)	ROA Coefficient (p value)	ROE Coefficient (p value)	LN_MC Coefficient (p value)	RDI Coefficient (p value)	AMI Coefficient (p value)	CI Coefficient (p value)
LN_ST	1.00						
ROA	0.8807*	1.00					
	0.000						
ROE	0.9298*	0.9910*	1.00				
	0.000	0.000					
LN_MC	0.9822*	0.8409*	0.8947*	1.00			
	0.000	0.000	0.000				
RDI	0.9254*	0.9920*	0.9991*	0.8899*	1.00		
	0.000	0.000	0.000	0.000			
AMI	−0.4327*	−0.6568*	−0.6209*	−0.3576*	−0.6236*	1.00	
	0.000	0.000	0.000	0.000	0.000		
CI	−0.2083*	−0.3115*	−0.2912*	−0.0961*	−0.2920*	−0.4262*	1.00
	0.000	0.000	0.000	0.0247	0.000	0.000	
LR	−0.1221*	−0.1452*	−0.1335*	−0.072	−0.1336*	−0.2340*	0.3056*
	0.0043	0.0007	0.0018	0.0927	0.0018	0.000	0.000
OER	−0.3716*	−0.4880*	−0.4758*	−0.2767*	−0.4751*	−0.6481*	0.6092*
	0.000	0.000	0.000	0.000	0.000	0.000	0.000

*Denotes at 5% level of significance
Source Author's own
Software used Stata Software (version 12)

and Control Variables (CV) are AMI, CI, LR and OR. No serial correlation was found in the well-balanced dataset because all the correlation coefficients are matrix <0.80 of the above-mentioned bisexual relationship. We can find a statistically significant positive correlation between Ln_ST and RDI. All the Control Variables AMI, CI, LR and OER have statistically negative significant correlation with Ln_ST. All other financial performance Dependent Variables (ROA, ROE and LN_MC) like Ln_ST have statistically significant positive correlations with RDI. In this bivariate correlation matrix, we observed statistically significant negative correlations between all Control Variables AMI, CI, LR, OER and financial performance Dependent Variables (ROA, ROE and Ln_MC). All coefficient estimates are statistically significant at 5% level. Overall, this bivariate correlation matrix is favourable for the study.

7.11.3   Diagnostic Tests: VIF & SK Test

a. **Variation Inflation Factor (VIF)**

From Table 7.7, we find that the VIF values of RDI, AMI, CI, LR and OER are 1.66, 2.25, 1.67, 1.12 and 2.28, respectively. All VIF values are below (<) 4 and nowhere near to the rule of thumb (maximum acceptable cut-off value for the VIF is 10 and minimum cut-off value for tolerance, i.e. 1/VIF is 0.10. Literature is available according to different econometrics). All variables RDI, AMI, CI, LR and OR will be considered for this study as all these variables are free from multiple according to VIF results.

b. **Skewness/Kurtosis Tests for Normality**

From Table 7.8, we can find the results of Skewness/Kurtosis Tests related to all the practice models for use in the panel regression

Table 7.7 VIF result of Category-A companies

Independent/control variables	VIF	1/VIF
RDI	1.66	0.601778
AMI	2.25	0.444943
CI	1.67	0.599638
LR	1.12	0.892887
OER	2.28	0.438468

Source Author's own calculation in Stata Software (version 12)

Table 7.8   Test for Normality of Category-A companies

Test name	Purpose of the test	Null hypothesis (H_0)	Alternative hypothesis (H_1)	Test statistic	Result
Skewness/Kurtosis tests for normality	To check the normality of the sample data set	Normal Distribution	Not Normal Distribution	p value of test statistic is greater than 0.05 in all empirical models (I, II, III and IV)	Normal Distribution for all empirical models (I, II, III and IV)

Source Author's own calculation in Stata Software (version 12)

model for generality. In the case of the four regression models associated with the section: A Company, we can find out that the p value of χ^2 is greater than (>) 0.05 and the distribution is normal.

7.11.4   Empirical Model and Panel Regression Analysis of Company Category: A

After going through all the steps, Fixed Effect Model (FEM) and Random Effect Model (REM) have been applied taking all four (4) Dependent Variables (DV) Ln_ST, ROA, ROE and Ln_MC of this study one after another. At first, following Empirical Model by incorporating Ln_ST as Dependent Variable (DV) will be estimated.

Estimation of Empirical Model-1 of A Category Company

$$\text{Ln\_ST}_{it} = \alpha + \beta_{1it}\text{RDI}_{it} + \beta_{2it}\text{AMI}_{it} + \beta_{3it}\text{CI}_{it} + \beta_{4it}\text{LR}_{it} + \beta_{5it}\text{OER}_{it} + \text{\euro}_{it} \quad (7.5)$$

From Table 7.9, we can find panel data regression results for both Fixed Effect Model (FEM) and Random Effect Model (REM). Hausman Test has been used in the study to make a strong choice between the

Table 7.9 Panel regression results of Category-A company, model no. 1

Model/independent variables	FEM coefficients (p value)	REM coefficients (p value)
Constant	−2.12***	−2.15***
	(0.00)	(0.00)
RDI	10.33***	10.33***
	(0.00)	(0.00)
AMI	6.49***	6.61***
	(0.00)	(0.00)
CI	−0.188***	−0.185***
	(0.00)	(0.00)
LR	0.285**	0.276**
	(0.04)	(0.04)
OER	−0.052*	−0.051*
	(0.07)	(0.07)
F/χ^2	1315.13***	6930.69***
	(0.00)	(0.00)
R^2	0.8826	0.8831

***Denotes significant at 1%, **at 5% and *at 10% level of significance
Source Author's own calculation in Stata Software (version 12)

Fixed Effect Model (FEM) and the Random Effect Model (REM). The following shows the results of the Houseman Test:

Table 7.10 shows the result of Hausman Test. From the above-mentioned table, we can visualize the p value of χ^2 is 0.59 which is greater than (>) 0.05 or 5%. Since p value of χ^2 is greater than (>) 0.05 or 5%, the result is statistically insignificant and the Null Hypothesis (H_0) is accepted and the Alternate Hypothesis (H_1) is rejected. Finally, Random Effect Model (REM) is found to be most appropriate for the panel dataset used in this study.

The results of Random Effect Model (REM) are furnished in the following.

The value of χ^2 is 6930.69 and its corresponding p value is 0.00 (<0.05) which means that the model is good fit for interpretation. The value of R^2 is 0.8831. It signifies that the model can predict 88.31% variability. Explanatory Variable: RDI and Control Variable: AMI have positive effect on Ln_ST and both of their effects are statistically significant at 1% level. Control Variable: LR is also having positive effect on Ln_ST, but the effect is statistically significant at 5% level. There is a negative effect observed in case of Control Variable: CI on Ln_ST. But the effect is statistically significant at 1% level. Control Variable: OER is

Table 7.10   Hausman Test results of Category-A company, model no. 1

Test name	Purpose of the test	Null hypothesis (H_0)	Alternate hypothesis (H_1)	Test statistic	Preferred model as per Hausman Test
Hausman Test	To select the preferred model between Fixed Effect Model (FEM) and Random Effect Model (REM)	Random Effect Model (REM) is appropriate	Fixed Effect Model (FEM) is appropriate	Prob > χ^2 (5) = 0.59	Random Effect Model (REM)

Source Author's own calculation in Stata Software (version 12)

having negative effect on Ln_ST, but the effect is statistically significant at 10% level.

Estimation of Empirical Model-2 of A Category Company

Now, an attempt has been taken to estimate the following regression model.

$$\text{ROA}_{it} = \alpha + \beta_{1it}\text{RDI}_{it} + \beta_{2it}\text{AMI}_{it} + \beta_{3it}\text{CI}_{it} + \beta_{4it}\text{LR}_{it} + \beta_{5it}\text{OER}_{it} + \text{\euro}_{it} \qquad (7.6)$$

The following table shows the result of panel regression analysis taking Return on Assets (ROA) as Dependent Variable.

From Table 7.11, we can find panel data regression results for both Fixed Effect Model (FEM) and Random Effect Model (REM). Hausman Test has been estimated in order to have a robust selection between Fixed Effect Model (FEM) and Random Effect Model (REM). In the following table, the result of Hausman Test is shown.

Table 7.12 shows the result of Hausman Test. From the above-mentioned table, we come to know the p value of χ^2 is 0.00 which is less than (<) 0.05 or 5%. Since p value of χ^2 is less than (<) 0.05 or 5%, the result is statistically significant and the Null Hypothesis (H_0) is rejected and the Alternate Hypothesis (H_1) is accepted. Finally, Fixed

Table 7.11 Panel regression results of Category-A company, model no. 2

Model/independent variables	FEM coefficients (p value)	REM coefficients (p value)
Constant	−0.408	−0.409
	0.00	0.00
RDI	1.31***	1.31***
	0.00	0.00
AMI	−0.257***	−0.258
	0.00	0.00
CI	0.009***	0.009***
	0.00	0.00
LR	−0.021***	−0.021
	0.01	0.01
OER	0.001	0.001
	0.47	0.45
F/χ^2	5293.43***	28,339.57***
	0.00	0.00
R^2	0.9859	0.9859

***Denotes significant at 1%, **at 5% and *at 10% level of significance
Source Author's own calculation in Stata Software (version 12)

Table 7.12 Hausman Test results of Category-A company, model no. 2

Test name	Purpose of the test	Null hypothesis (H_0)	Alternate hypothesis (H_1)	Test statistic	Preferred model as per Hausman Test
Hausman Test	To select the preferred model between Fixed Effect Model (FEM) and Random Effect Model (REM)	Random Effect Model (REM) is appropriate	Fixed Effect Model (FEM) is appropriate	Prob < χ^2 (5) = 0.00	Fixed Effect Model (FEM)

Source Author's own calculation in Stata Software (version 12)

Effect Model (FEM) is found to be most appropriate for the panel dataset used in this study.

The results of Fixed Effect Model (FEM) are shown in the following.

The value of F Statistics is 5293.43 and its relative p value is 0.00 which is less than (<) 0.05. This means the model is good for study. The value of R^2 is 0.9859 which indicates that the model can explain 98.59% variability. Independent Variable: RDI is having positive effect on ROA and its effect is statistically significant at 1% level. Control Variables: CIA and ROA have a positive effect and this effect is statistically significant at the 1% level. Both Control Variables: AMI and LR have a negative effect on the ROA, but both of their effects are statistically significant at the 1% level. Control Variable: OER has a positive effect on ROA but its effect is not statistically significant because the p value of OER is 0.479 which is more than 10% of the instant.

Estimation of Empirical Model-3 of A Category Company

In this, an effort has been taken to estimate the following panel data regression analysis by incorporating Return on Equity (ROE) as Dependent Variable.

$$\text{ROE}_{it} = \alpha + \beta_{1it}\text{RDI}_{it} + \beta_{2it}\text{AMI}_{it} + \beta_{3it}\text{CI}_{it} + \beta_{4it}\text{LR}_{it} + \beta_{5it}\text{OER}_{it} + \epsilon_{it} \qquad (7.7)$$

From Table 7.13, we can find panel data regression results for both Fixed Effect Model (FEM) and Random Effect Model (REM). Hausman Test has been estimated in order to have a robust selection between Fixed Effect Model (FEM) and Random Effect Model (REM). In the following table, the result of Hausman Test is shown.

Table 7.14 shows the result of Hausman Test. From above-mentioned table, we can see the p value of χ^2 is 0.00 which is less than (<) 0.05 or 5%. Since p value of χ^2 is <0.05 or 5%, the result is statistically significant and the Null Hypothesis (H_0) is rejected and the Alternate Hypothesis (H_1) is accepted. Finally, the Fixed Impact Model (FEM) seems to be the most suitable for the panel dataset used in this study.

The results of Fixed Effect Model (FEM) are shown in the following.

The value of F Statistics is 6127.28 and its corresponding p value is 0.00 which is <0.05. This means that the model is good fit for study. The value of R^2 is 0.9982 which indicates that the model can explain 99.82% variability. Independent Variable: RDI is having a positive effect on ROE and its effect is statistically significant at 1% level. Control Variable: AMI has a positive effect on ROE and is statistically significant at the 5% level.

Table 7.13 Panel regression results of Category-A company, model no. 3

Model/independent variables	FEM coefficients (p value)	REM coefficients (p value)
Constant	−0.009	−0.006
	(0.36)	(0.23)
RDI	0.99***	1.00***
	(0.00)	(0.00)
AMI	0.05**	0.018
	(0.05)	(0.12)
CI	0.00	0.000
	(0.67)	(0.55)
LR	0.00*	0.00
	(0.09)	(0.10)
OER	−0.00	−0.001
	(0.37)	(0.13)
F/χ^2	6127.28***	161,214.24***
	(0.00)	(0.00)
R^2	0.9982	0.9982

***Denotes significant at 1%, **at 5% and *at 10% level of significance
Source Author's own calculation in Stata Software (version 12)

Table 7.14 Hausman Test results of Category-A company, model no. 3

Test name	Purpose of the test	Null hypothesis (H_0)	Alternate hypothesis (H_1)	Test statistic	Preferred model as per Hausman Test
Hausman Test	To select the preferred model between Fixed Effect Model (FEM) and Random Effect Model (REM)	Random Effect Model (REM) is appropriate	Fixed Effect Model (FEM) is appropriate	Prob < χ^2 (5) = 0.00	Fixed Effect Model (FEM)

Source Author's own calculation in Stata Software (version 12)

Control Variable: CI has a positive effect on ROE, but the effect is statistically insignificant. Control Variable: LR is having a significant effect on ROE and is statistically significant at 10% level. Control Variable: OER has a negative impact on ROE and its impact is not statistically insignificant.

Estimation of Empirical Model-4 of A Category Company

Now, following panel data regression analysis has been estimated by incorporating Ln_MC as Dependent Variable.

$$Ln\_MC_{it} = \alpha + \beta_{1it}RDI_{it} + \beta_{2it}AMI_{it} + \beta_{3it}CI_{it} + \beta_{4it}LR_{it} + \beta_{5it}OER_{it} + \epsilon_{it} \quad (7.8)$$

From Table 7.15, we can find panel data regression results for both Fixed Effect Model (FEM) and Random Effect Model (REM). Hausman Test has been estimated in order to have a robust selection between Fixed Effect Model (FEM) and Random Effect Model (REM). In the following table, the result of Hausman Test is shown.

Table 7.16 shows the result of Hausman Test. From the above-mentioned table, we come to know the p value of χ^2 is 0.0460 which is <0.05 or 5%. Since p value of χ^2 is <0.05 or 5%, the result is statistically significant and the Null Hypothesis (H_0) is rejected and the Alternate

Table 7.15 Panel regression results Category-A company, model no. 4	*Model/independent variables*	*FEM coefficients (p value)*	*REM coefficients (p value)*
	Constant	−1.76 (0.00)	−1.89 (0.00)
	RDI	10.51*** (0.00)	10.47*** (0.00)
	AMI	6.88*** (0.00)	7.35*** (0.00)
	CI	4.02** (0.02)	−0.01 (0.68)
	LR	0.26 (0.21)	0.27 (0.18)
	OER	0.09** (0.03)	0.09** (0.02)
	F/χ^2	595.90*** (0.00)	3113.67*** (0.00)
	R^2	0.8451	0.8478

***Denotes significant at 1%, **at 5% and *at 10% level of significance
Source Author's own calculation in Stata Software (version 12)

Table 7.16 Hausman Test results Category-A company, model no. 4

Test name	Purpose of the test	Null hypothesis (H_0)	Alternate hypothesis (H_1)	Test statistic	Preferred model as per Hausman Test
Hausman Test	To select the preferred model between Fixed Effect Model (FEM) and Random Effect Model (REM)	Random Effect Model (REM) is appropriate	Fixed Effect Model (FEM) is appropriate	Prob < χ^2 (5) = 0.0460	Fixed Effect Model (FEM)

Source Author's own calculation in Stata Software (version 12)

Hypothesis (H_1) is accepted. Finally, Fixed Effect Model (FEM) is found to be most appropriate for Empirical Model-4.

The results of Fixed Effect Model (FEM) are shown in the following. The value of F Statistics is 595.90 and its corresponding p value is 0.00 which is <0.05. This implies that the model is a suitable fit for study. The value of R^2 is 0.8451. This indicates that the model can predict 84.51% variability. Explanatory Variable: RDI and Control Variable: AMI have a positive effect on Ln_MC and both of their effects are statistically significant at 1% level. Control Variable: CI has a positive effect on Ln_MC and the effect is statistically significant at 5% level. The Control Variable: LR has a positive effect on Ln_MC, but the effect is not statistically insignificant. Control Variable: OER is having a positive effect on Ln_MC and the effect is statistically significant at the 5% level.

Table 7.17 provides the summarized panel regression results for four (4) empirical models of all the Dependent Variables (DV): Ln_ST, ROA, ROE and Ln_MC based on the appropriate model as per Hausman Test of Category: A pharmaceutical companies.

Table 7.17 Summarized panel regression results of 4 empirical models of Category: A company

Independent Variables	Dependent variable for empirical model #1 Ln_ST REM Coefficients (p value)	Dependent variable for empirical model #2 ROA FEM Coefficients (p value)	Dependent variable for empirical model #3 ROE FEM Coefficients (p value)	Dependent variable for empirical model #4 Ln_MC FEM Coefficients (p value)
Constant	−2.15*** (0.00)	−0.408 0.00	−0.009 (0.36)	−1.76 (0.00)
RDI	10.33*** (0.00)	1.31*** 0.00	0.99*** (0.00)	10.51*** (0.00)
AMI	6.61*** (0.00)	−0.257*** 0.00	0.05** (0.05)	6.88*** (0.00)
CI	−0.185*** (0.00)	0.009*** 0.00	0.00 (0.67)	4.02** (0.02)
LR	0.276** (0.04)	−0.021*** 0.01	0.00* (0.09)	0.26 (0.21)
OER	−0.051* (0.07)	0.001 0.47	−0.00 (0.37)	0.09** (0.03)
F/χ^2	6930.69*** (0.00)	5293.43 0.00	6127.28 (0.00)	595.90*** (0.00)
R^2	0.8831	0.9859	0.9982	0.8451

***Denotes significant at 1%, **at 5% and *at 10% level of significance
Source Author's own calculation in Stata Software (version 12)

7.12   Empirical Study of Company Category: B

In this section, a discussion has been made with regard to the impact of research and development activities of Company Type: B which is consisting with National Stock Exchange (NSE)-listed Indian pharmaceutical companies having turnover more than three hundred crores (>₹300).

The list of the Category-B companies is furnished in the following table.

From Table 7.18, we can find out the names of Category-B companies taken for empirical study. In the following, detailed empirical analysis for Company Category: B is discussed.

Table 7.18 List of Category-B companies

Sl. no	Company name	Sl. no	Company name
1	Sun Pharmaceutical Industries Limited	20	Granules India Limited
2	Cadila Healthcare Limited	21	Strides Shasun Limited
3	Piramal Enterprises Limited	22	Eris Lifesciences Limited
4	Cipla Limited	23	Wockhardt Limited
5	Lupin Limited	24	Ipca Laboratories Limited
6	Aurobindo Pharma Limited	25	Dr Lal Paths Lab Limited
7	Dr Reddy Laboratory Limited	26	Laurus Labs Limited
8	Divi's Laboratories Limited	27	Caplin Point Laboratories Limited
9	Alkem Laboratories Limited	28	Shilpa Medicare Limited
10	Torrent Pharmaceuticals Limited	29	FDC Limited
11	Biocon Limited	30	Advanced Enzyme
12	Ajanta Pharma Limited	31	Twilight Litaka Pharma Ltd
13	Glenmark Pharmaceutical Limited	32	SeQuent Scientific Limited
14	Natco Pharma Limited	33	Vinati Organics Limited
15	Jubilant Life Sciences Limited	34	Wanbury Limited
16	Alembic Pharmaceuticals Limited	35	Morepen Laboratories Limited
17	Unichem Laboratories Limited	36	IND Swift Limited
18	Suven Life Sciences Limited	37	Elder Pharmaceuticals Limited
19	JB Chemicals and Pharmaceuticals Limited		

Source Author's own

7.12.1 *Descriptive Statistics*

With the help of descriptive statistics, we can also learn simple summaries about samples and arrangements.

Table 7.19 lists 777 observations covering 21 periods (from 1995 to 2015) #37 NSE-listed Indian pharmaceutical companies. The average amount of R&D Expenditure (Independent Variable: RDI) deployed by the sample pharmaceutical companies is 1.75 crore. There is a wide variation in research and development expenditure with a minimum of Rs 0.52 crore and a maximum of Rs 5.6 crore.

This dispersion is also supported by 1.08 crore standard deviation. We can observe that the sample companies are incurring on an average 1.72 crores in the areas of Advertising and Marketing Expenditure (Control Variable: AMI). In the case of AMI, the values are minimum 0.01 crore and maximum 8.38 crore where the standard deviation is spread by 1.15 crore.

Table 7.19 Descriptive statistics of Category-B companies

Variable	Obs	Mean	Std. Dev	Min	Max
LN_ST (₹ Cr.)	777	1.533295	0.3141782	0.88	2.53
ROA (%)	777	0.8838996	0.5453308	−0.26	2.95
ROE (%)	777	1.894337	0.5600965	0.69	3.88
LN_MC (₹ Cr.)	777	1.452355	0.295993	0.82	2.4
RDI (%)	777	1.75964	1.085971	−0.52	5.88
AMI (%)	777	1.722857	1.187308	0.01	8.38
CI (%)	777	1.741519	1.826288	0.01	17.54
LR (%)	777	1.746049	1.070883	−0.52	5.88
OER (%)	777	1.805444	3.881467	0.03	42.06

Source Author's own calculation in Stata Software (version 12)

The average amount of Capital Intensity (Control Variable: CI) employed by the sample companies is 1.74 crores. CI values are also spread where the minimum is 0.01 crore and the maximum is 17.54 crore and this dispersion supports 1.82 crore with the ideal deviation. Sample pharmaceutical companies use a Leverage Ratio (Control Variable: LR) with an average of 1.74. Scattering is observed in LR cases where minimum −0.52 and maximum 88.6 and this scattering is supported by the standard deviation 1.07. Sample pharmaceutical companies have set an operating cost (Control Variable: OER) with an average cost of Rs 1.80 crore, and this cost is very wide where minimum cost is Rs 0.03 crore and maximum cost is Rs 42.06 crore.

The spread of this OER expenditure is also supported by standard deviation 3.88 crore. The average Sales Turnover (Dependent Variable: Ln_ST) clocked by the sample pharmaceutical companies is 1.53 crore. The Return on Assets (Dependent Variable: ROA) is 88.38% for the study period where the Return on Equity (Dependent Variable: ROE) is 1.89. The sample pharmaceutical companies have achieved average Market Capitalization (Dependent Variable: Ln_MC) of 1.45 crore. This Market Capitalization of the sample companies is very much spread where the minimum Market Capitalization is 0.82 crore and the maximum Market Capitalization is 2.4 crore. This dispersion is supported by standard deviation of 0.29.

7.12.2 Bivariate Correlation Matrix

The Bivariate Correlation Matrix pertaining to B Category pharmaceutical companies is presented below.

From the Bivariate Correlation Matrix presented in Table 7.20, we can find the bivariate correlation between Dependent Variable verses Independent Variable and Control Variables. In this bivariate correlation matrix, financial performance-related dependent variables (DV) are Ln_ST, ROA, ROE and Ln_MC, RDI is an Independent Variable (IV) and the Control Variables (CV) are AMI, CI, LR and OER. After reading the mentioned bivariate correlation matrix <0.80 on this strongly balanced dataset, not all correlation coefficients were found. We can observe the statistically significant positive correlation between Ln_ST and RDI, AMI, CI, LR and OER. Dependent Variable: ROA is having significant positive correlation with RDI, AMI, CI, LR and OER. Independent Variable: RDI and Control Variables: AMI, CI, LR and OER are having statistically significant positive correlation with ROE. At last, we can further observe that like Ln_ST, ROA and ROE financial performance-related variables, Ln_MC is also having statistically significant positive correlation with RDI, AMI, CI, LR and OER. All coefficient estimates are statistically significant at 5% level. Overall, this bivariate correlation matrix is favourable for the study.

7.12.3 Diagnostic Tests: VIF & SK Test

a. **Variation Inflation Factor (VIF)**

From Table 7.21, we have observed the VIF values of RDI, AMI, CI, LR and OER are 2.35, 1.66, 1.26, 1.80 and 1.12, respectively. All VIF values are below (<) 4 and are nowhere near to the rule of thumb (the most acceptable cut-off value for the VIF is 10 and minimum cut-off price for tolerance, i.e. 1/VIF, is 0.10 which is available in various econometric literatures). All variables RDI, AMI, CI, LR and OER will be considered for this study as all these variables are free from multicollinearity as per VIF result related to Category: B Company.

b. **Skewness/Kurtosis Tests for Normality**

From Table 7.22, we find the results of Skewness/Kurtosis Tests for normality pertain to all empirical models to be used in this panel regression model. In the case of four regression models associated with Category: B Company, we can find out that the p value of χ^2 is greater than (>) 0.05 and the distribution is normal.

Table 7.20 Bivariate correlation matrix of Category-B companies

Variables	LN_ST Coefficient (p value)	ROA Coefficient (p value)	ROE Coefficient (p value)	LN_MC Coefficient (p value)	RDI Coefficient (p value)	AMI Coefficient (p value)	CI Coefficient (p value)
LN_ST	1						
ROA	0.8916* 0	1					
ROE	0.9589* 0	0.9834* 0	1				
LN_MC	0.9927* 0	0.9394* 0	0.9859* 0	1			
RDI	0.8915* 0	1.0000* 0	0.9834* 0	0.9394* 0	1		
AMI	0.6965* 0	0.6079* 0	0.6595* 0	0.6883* 0	0.6076* 0	1	
CI	0.4629* 0	0.2871* 0	0.3652* 0	0.4255* 0	0.2870* 0	0.3257* 0	1
LR	0.5990* 0	0.6654* 0	0.6564* 0	0.6292* 0	0.6652* 0	0.4334* 0	0.1777* 0
OER	0.2971* 0	0.0722* 0.0443	0.1639* 0	0.2432* 0	0.0722* 0.0441	0.0714* 0.0467	0.3243* 0

*Denotes at 5% level of significance
Source Author's own calculation in Stata Software (version 12)

Table 7.21 VIF result of Category-B companies

Independent/control variables	VIF	1/VIF
RDI	2.35	0.426286
AMI	1.66	0.603563
CI	1.26	0.792004
LR	1.80	0.555643
OER	1.12	0.893539

Source Author's own calculation in Stata Software (version 12)

Table 7.22 Test for Normality of Category-B companies

Test name	Purpose of the test	Null hypothesis (H_0)	Alternative hypothesis (H_1)	Test statistic	Result
Skewness/Kurtosis Tests for Normality	To check the normality of the sample data set	Normal Distribution	Not Normal Distribution	p value of test statistic is greater than 0.05 in all empirical models (I, II, III and IV)	Normal Distribution for all empirical models (I, II, III and IV)

Source Author's own calculation in Stata Software (version 12)

7.12.4 Empirical Model and Panel Data Multivariate Regression Analysis

Estimation of Empirical Model-1 of B Category Company

Empirical Model:

$$Ln\_ST_{it} = \alpha + \beta_{1it}RDI_{it} + \beta_{2it}AMI_{it} + \beta_{3it}CI_{it}$$
$$+\beta_{4it}LR_{it} + \beta_{5it}OER_{it} + \in_{it} \tag{7.9}$$

From Table 7.23, we can find panel data regression results for both Fixed Effect Model (FEM) and Random Effect Model (REM). Hausman Test

Table 7.23   Panel regression results of Category-B companies, model no. 1

Model/independent variables	FEM coefficients (p value)	REM coefficients (p value)
Constant	1.06***	1.05***
	(0.00)	(0.00)
RDI	0.21***	0.21***
	(0.00)	(0.00)
AMI	0.02***	0.02***
	(0.00)	(0.00)
CI	0.01***	0.01***
	(0.00)	(0.00)
LR	−0.00***	−0.00
	(0.06)	(0.12)
OER	0.01***	0.01***
	(0.00)	(0.00)
F/χ^2	1008.61***	5349.92***
	(0.00)	(0.00)
R^2	0.8894	0.8906

***Denotes significant at 1%, **at 5% and *at 10% level of significance
Source Author's own calculation in Stata Software (version 12)

has been estimated in order to have a robust selection between Fixed Effect Model (FEM) and Random Effect Model (REM). In the following table, the result of Hausman Test is shown.

Table 7.24 shows the result of Hausman Test. From the above-mentioned table, we come to know the p value of χ^2 is 0.00 which is less than (<) 0.05 or 5%. Since p value of χ^2 is less than (<) 0.05 or 5%, the result is statistically significant and the Null Hypothesis (H_0) is rejected and the Alternate Hypothesis (H_1) is accepted. Finally, Fixed Effect Model (FEM) seems to be the most suitable for the panel dataset used in this study.

The results of Fixed Effect Model (FEM) are shown in the following.

The value of F Statistics is 1008.61 and the corresponding p value is 0.00 which is less than (<) 0.05. This means the model is good for study. The value of R^2 is 0.8894 which indicates that the model can explain 88.94% variability. Independent Variable: RDI is having positive effect on Ln_ST and its effect is statistically significant at the 1% level. Control Variables: AMI, CI and OER have a positive effect on Ln_ST and the effect is statistically significant at 1% level. Control Variable: LR has a negative effect on Ln_ST, but the effect is statistically significant at 10% level.

Table 7.24 Hausman test results of Category-B companies, model no. 1

Test name	Purpose of the test	Null hypothesis (H_0)	Alternate hypothesis (H_1)	Test statistic	Preferred model as per Hausman Test
Hausman Test	To select the preferred model between Fixed Effect Model (FEM) and Random Effect Model (REM)	Random Effect Model (REM) is appropriate	Fixed Effect Model (FEM) is appropriate	Prob < χ^2 (5) = 0.00	Fixed Effect Model (FEM)

Source Author's own calculation in Stata Software (version 12)

Estimation of Empirical Model-2 of B Category Company

Now, following regression model will be estimated.

$$\text{ROA}_{it} = \alpha + \beta_{1it}\text{RDI}_{it} + \beta_{2it}\text{AMI}_{it} + \beta_{3it}\text{CI}_{it} + \beta_{4it}\text{LR}_{it} + \beta_{5it}\text{OER}_{it} + \in_{it} \quad (7.10)$$

The following table shows the result of panel regression analysis taking Return on Assets (ROA) as Dependent Variable.

From Table 7.25, we can find panel data regression results for both Fixed Effect Model (FEM) and Random Effect Model (REM) under Empirical Model-2. Hausman Test has been estimated in order to have a robust selection between Fixed Effect Model (FEM) and Random Effect Model (REM). In the following table, the result of Hausman Test is shown.

Table 7.26 shows the result of Hausman Test. From the table above, we can visualize the p value of χ^2 is 0.09 which is greater than (>) 0.05 or 5%. Since p value of χ^2 is greater than (>) 0.05, the answer is statistically trivial and the Null Hypothesis (H_0) is recognized and the Alternate Hypothesis (H_1) is rejected. Finally, the Random Effect Model (REM) seems to be the most suitable for the panel dataset used in this study.

The results of Random Effect Model (REM) are furnished in the following.

Table 7.25 Panel regression results of Category-B companies, model no. 2

Model/independent variables	FEM coefficients (p value)	REM coefficients (p value)
Constant	0.00 (0.50)	0.00 (0.60)
RDI	0.50*** (0.00)	**0.50*** (0.00)**
AMI	0.00 (0.25)	0.00 (0.14)
CI	3.37 (0.09)	**3.74** (0.08)**
LR	0.00 (0.44)	0.00 (0.39)
OER	0.00 (0.43)	0.00 (0.64)
F/χ^2	2.20*** (0.00)	**1.48*** (0.00)**
R^2	1.00	1.00

***Denotes significant at 1%, **at 5% and *at 10% level of significance
Source Author's own calculation in Stata Software (version 12)

Table 7.26 Hausman Test results of Category-B companies, model no. 2

Test name	Purpose of the test	Null hypothesis (H_0)	Alternate hypothesis (H_1)	Test statistic	Preferred model as per Hausman Test
Hausman Test	To select the preferred model between Fixed Effect Model (FEM) and Random Effect Model (REM)	Random Effect Model (REM) is appropriate	Fixed Effect Model (FEM) is appropriate	Prob > χ^2 (5) = 0.09	Random Effect Model (REM)

Source Author's own calculation in Stata Software (version 12)

The value of χ^2 is 1.48 and the corresponding p value is 0.00 (<0.05) which means the model is good fit for interpretation. The value of R^2

is 1.00. It indicates the model can predict 100% variability. Explanatory Variable: RDI is having positive effect on ROA and the effect is statistically significant at 1% level. We have found that Control Variable: CI has a positive effect on ROA and its effect is statistically significant at 10% level. We further noted that all Control Variables: AMI, LR and OER have a positive effect on Return on Assets (ROA), but the effect is not statistically significant.

Estimation of Empirical Model-3 of B Category Company

In this section, following panel data regression analysis has been estimated by incorporating Return on Equity (ROE) as Dependent Variable.

$$ROE_{it} = \alpha + \beta_{1it}RDI_{it} + \beta_{2it}AMI_{it} + \beta_{3it}CI_{it} + \beta_{4it}LR_{it} + \beta_{5it}OER_{it} + \varepsilon_{it} \quad (7.11)$$

From Table 7.27, we can find panel data regression results for both Fixed Effect Model (FEM) and Random Effect Model (REM) under Empirical Model-3. Hausman Test has been estimated in order to have a robust

Table 7.27 Panel regression results of Category-B companies, model no. 3

Model/independent variables	FEM coefficients (p value)	REM coefficients (p value)
Constant	0.98***	0.98***
	(0.00)	(0.00)
RDI	0.47***	0.47***
	(0.00)	(0.00)
AMI	0.01***	0.02***
	(0.00)	(0.00)
CI	0.01***	0.01***
	(0.00)	(0.00)
LR	−0.00*	−0.00
	(0.06)	(0.12)
OER	0.00***	0.00***
	(0.00)	(0.00)
F/χ^2	8025.62***	42,015.40***
	(0.00)	(0.00)
R^2	0.9820	0.9822

***Denotes significant at 1%, **at 5% and *10% level of significance
Source Author's own calculation in Stata Software (version 12)

selection between Fixed Effect Model (FEM) and Random Effect Model (REM). In the following table, the result of Hausman Test is shown.

Table 7.28 shows the result of Hausman Test. From the table above, we can see the p value of χ^2 is 0.00 which is less than (<) 0.05 or 5%. Since p value of χ^2 is <0.05 or 5%, the result is statistically significant and the Null Hypothesis (H_0) is rejected and the Alternate Hypothesis (H_1) is accepted. Finally, Fixed Effect Model (FEM) seems to be most suitable for the panel dataset used in this study.

The results of Fixed Effect Model (FEM) are shown in the following.

The value of F Statistics is 8025.62 and its corresponding p value is 0.00 which is <0.05. This means that the model is good for study. The value of R^2 is 0.9820 which shows that the model can explain 98.20% variability. Independent Variable: RDI has a positive effect on ROE and its effect is statistically significant at the 1% level. Control Variables: AMI, CI and OER have positive effect on ROE and the effect is statistically significant at 1% level. We also found that Control Variable: LR has a negative effect on ROE, but the effect is statically significant at the 10% level.

Table 7.28   Hausman Test results of Category-B companies, model no. 3

Test name	Purpose of the test	Null hypothesis (H_0)	Alternate hypothesis (H_1)	Test statistic	Preferred model as per Hausman Test
Hausman Test	To select the preferred model between Fixed Effect Model (FEM) and Random Effect Model (REM)	Random Effect Model (REM) is appropriate	Fixed Effect Model (FEM) is appropriate	Prob < χ^2 (5) = 0.00	Fixed Effect Model (FEM)

Source Author's own calculation in Stata Software (version 12)

Estimation of Empirical Model-4 of B Category Company

In this section, panel data regression analysis will be estimated by incorporating Ln_MC as Dependent Variable.

$$Ln\_MC_{it} = \alpha + \beta_{1it}RDI_{it} + \beta_{2it}AMI_{it} + \beta_{3it}CI_{it} + \beta_{4it}LR_{it}$$
$$+ \beta_{5it}OER_{it} + \epsilon_{it} \qquad (7.12)$$

From Table 7.29, we can find panel data regression results for both Fixed Effect Model (FEM) and Random Effect Model (REM) under Empirical Model-4. Hausman Test has been estimated in order to have a robust selection between Fixed Effect Model (FEM) and Random Effect Model (REM). In the following table, the result of Hausman Test is shown.

Table 7.30 shows the result of Hausman Test. From the table above, we can see the p value of χ^2 is 0.00 which is less than (<) 0.05 or 5%. Since p value of χ^2 is <0.05 or 5%, the results are statistically significant and the Null Hypothesis (H_0) is rejected and the Alternate Hypothesis (H_1) is accepted. Finally, Fixed Effect Model (FEM) seems to be most suitable for the panel dataset used in this study.

The results of Fixed Effect Model (FEM) are shown in the following.

Table 7.29 Panel regression results of Category-B companies, model no. 4

Model/independent variables	FEM coefficients (p value)	REM coefficients (p value)
Constant	0.99***	0.98***
	(0.00)	(0.00)
RDI	0.22***	0.22***
	(0.00)	(0.00)
AMI	0.01***	0.02***
	(0.00)	(0.00)
CI	0.01***	0.01***
	(0.00)	(0.00)
LR	−0.00**	−0.00*
	(0.05)	(0.09)
OER	0.00***	0.00***
	(0.00)	(0.00)
F/χ^2	1980.54***	10,433.77***
	(0.00)	(0.00)
R^2	0.9359	0.9367

Source Author's own calculation in Stata Software (version 12)

Table 7.30   Hausman Test results of Category-B companies, model no. 4

Test name	Purpose of the test	Null hypothesis (H_0)	Alternate hypothesis (H_1)	Test statistic	Preferred model as per Hausman Test
Hausman Test	To select the preferred model between Fixed Effect Model (FEM) and Random Effect Model (REM)	Random Effect Model (REM) is appropriate	Fixed Effect Model (FEM) is appropriate	Prob < χ^2 (5) = 0.00	Fixed Effect Model (FEM)

Source Author's own calculation in Stata Software (version 12)

The value of F Statistics is 1980.54 and the corresponding p value is 0.00 which is <0.05. This means that the model is suitable for study. The value of R^2 is 0.9359 which indicates that the model can explain 93.59% variability. Explanatory Variable: RDI is having a positive effect on Ln_MC and the effect is statistically significant at 1% level. It has also been found that Control Variables: AMI, CI and OER are having positive effect on Ln_MC and the effect is statistically significant at 1% level. It has been observed that Control Variable: LR is having negative effect on Ln_MC, but the effect is statistically significant at 5% level.

Table 7.31 provides the summarized panel regression results for four (4) empirical models of all the Dependent Variables (DV): Ln_ST, ROA, ROE and Ln_MC based on the appropriate model as per Hausman Test pertain to the Category-B pharmaceutical companies consisting with Indian pharmaceutical companies having turnover more than ₹300 Crores.

Table 7.31 Summarized panel regression results of 4 empirical models of Category: B company

Independent Variables	Dependent variable for empirical model #1 Ln_ST FEM Coefficients (p value)	Dependent variable for empirical model #2 ROA REM Coefficients (p value)	Dependent variable for empirical model #3 ROE FEM Coefficients (p value)	Dependent variable for empirical model #4 Ln_MC FEM Coefficients (p value)
Constant	1.06*** (0.00)	0.00 (0.60)	0.98*** (0.00)	0.99*** (0.00)
RDI	0.21*** (0.00)	0.50*** (0.00)	0.47*** (0.00)	0.22*** (0.00)
AMI	0.02*** (0.00)	0.00 (0.14)	0.01*** (0.00)	0.01*** (0.00)
CI	0.01*** (0.00)	3.74** (0.08)	0.01*** (0.00)	0.01*** (0.00)
LR	−0.00*** (0.06)	0.00 (0.39)	−0.00* (0.06)	−0.00** (0.05)
OER	0.01*** (0.00)	0.00 (0.64)	0.00*** (0.00)	0.00*** (0.00)
F/χ^2	1008.61*** (0.00)	1.48*** (0.00)	8025.62*** (0.00)	1980.54*** (0.00)
R^2	0.8894	1.00	0.9820	0.9359

***Denotes significant at 1%, **at 5% and *at 10% level of significance
Source Author's own calculation in Stata Software (version 12)

7.13 Combined Panel Regression Results of All Company Categories (A and B) Empirical Models

Combined panel regression results of this entire study is shown in the following.

Company Category-A = MNC Subsidiary Companies irrespective of any sales turnover
Company Category-B = Indian Pharmaceutical Companies having sales turnover more than 300 Crores (₹)
Ln_ST_{it} = Natural Logarithm of Sales Turnover
ROA_{it} = Return on Assets
ROE_{it} = Return on Equity

Ln_MC$_{it}$ = Natural Logarithm of Market Capitalization
RDI$_{it}$ = Research & Development Intensity
AMI$_{it}$ = Advertisement & Marketing Intensity
CI$_{it}$ = Capital Intensity
LR$_{it}$ = Leverage Ratio
OER$_{it}$ = Operating Expenditure to Total Assets Ratio
S = Significant (all significant results at 1%, 5% and 10% level denoted as 'S')
IS = Insignificant (all insignificant results denoted as 'IS')
1, 2, 3 and 4 = Empirical Model Numbers

From Table 7.32, at a glance we can observe the full empirical results of this study which deals with all category pharmaceutical companies (A and B) as well as all empirical models (4 models). The following is a brief discussion of the results of Significant ('S') and Insignificant ('IS') Empirical Test related to this study.

In the case of **Research and Development Intensity (RDI$_{it}$)**, it has been found that significant positive result in 8 cases, i.e. significant results in all cases.

The reasons in favour of significant result may be due to the following reasons.

Table 7.32 Combined panel regression results of Category-A and B companies

Company Category	Empirical Model	DV	RDI$_{it}$	AMI$_{it}$	CI$_{it}$	LR$_{it}$	OER$_{it}$
A	1	Ln_ST$_{it}$	S	S	S	S	S
A	2	ROA$_{it}$	S	S	S	S	IS
A	3	ROE$_{it}$	S	S	IS	S	IS
A	4	Ln_MC$_{it}$	S	S	S	IS	S
B	1	Ln_ST$_{it}$	S	S	S	S	S
B	2	ROA$_{it}$	S	IS	S	IS	IS
B	3	ROE$_{it}$	S	S	S	S	S
B	4	Ln_MC$_{it}$	S	S	S	S	S
Overall Significant Test Results = (Significant Results / Total Results)			08/08	07/08	07/08	06/08	05/08
Overall Variable-Wise Impact on Financial Performance based on Significant Test Results			100%	87.50%	87.50%	75.00%	62.50%

Source Conceptualized by the author

a. Inclination of the pharmaceutical companies for providing innovative healthcare solution and accordingly making adequate amount of investment in research and development (R&D) activities.
b. With this inclination for innovation, pharmaceutical companies can develop or introduce new healthcare solution, to serve the unmet healthcare needs of the patient fraternities at large in global context.
c. The innovative healthcare solution which is the outcome of research and development (R&D) activities may create new business areas or markets and form new profit growth which may impact and improve the financial performance of the pharmaceutical companies.
d. Sometimes this new profit growth in turn may support further research and development (R&D) expenditure and enable the pharmaceutical companies to enjoy the strategic advantage.
e. Innovative healthcare solution always gets attracted by global healthcare need to cater to the entire world for serving to the mankind.

In the case of *Advertising and Marketing Intensity (AMI$_{it}$)*, 7 out of 8 cases have shown significant positive effect on the financial conduct of the pharmaceutical companies of A & B category pharmaceutical companies.

The reason behind the significant positive impact may be due to the following reasons.

a. Proper planning of advertising and marketing (A&M) strategy with regard to innovative drug product which is the outcome of R&D activities.
b. Successful execution of marketing strategy which perhaps enabled the pharmaceutical companies to meet the bottom line and accomplish the organizational objective.
c. Managing the supply chain properly while delivering the innovative drug product to the people at large.

In this study, it has also been observed that in some specific cases, i.e., in case of B Category Company, there is an insignificant impact on Return on Assets (ROA) and it may be due to the following reasons.

a. Either poor advertising and marketing (A&M) strategy or delay in obtaining regulatory approval of innovative drug product or faulty product promotional techniques.
b. Poor execution of the advertisement planning.

In this study, it has been found that in case of *Capital Intensity (CI_{it})*, 7 cases out of 8 cases have shown significant impact on the financial performance. The reason of the significant result may be due to the following.

    a. The utilization of fixed assets in a systematic and scientific manner perhaps the reason for significant impact of Capital Intensity.
    b. Following relevant accounting norms and standard in appropriate manner during in the management of fixed assets.

This study has also revealed that in one (1) specific case, i.e. in case of A Category Company, there is an insignificant impact of Capital Intensity (CI_{it}) on Return on Equity (ROE) and the reason of insignificant may be due to the following.

    a. Failure in managing the fixed assets and charging high level of depreciation on fixed assets by the respective pharmaceutical companies.
    b. Under utilization of fixed assets during the study period.

This study has revealed 6 significant results out of 8 test results in case of *Leverage Ratio (LR_{it})*. These significant results of Leverage Ratio on the financial performance of pharmaceutical companies of A and B categories may be due to the following reasons.

    a. Managing the Leverage Ratio effectively by examining and understanding the overall debt load to equity.
    b. Following accounting standard followed by high degree of professionalism in the management of Leverage Ratio.

But in two specific categories, i.e. in case of A category pharmaceutical company on Market Capitalization (Ln_MC) and in case of B category pharmaceutical company, Return on Assets (ROA); the impact of Leverage Ratio (LR_{it}) has been found as insignificant and it may be due to the following reasons.

    a. Either creditors having an equal or more stakes in the business assets of the different pharmaceutical companies considered for this study.

b. Paying high interest rate while sourcing of the debt from the financial institutions/money lending agencies.

c. Absence of efficient fund manager or sourcing capital from wrong sources.

d. Putting more emphasis on debt fund rather than equity.

At the end of the study, we can notice that in case of **Operating Expenditure to the Total Assets Ratio (OER$_{it}$)**, 5 cases have shown the significant test results on the financial performance of the pharmaceutical companies and it may be due to the following reasons.

a. Most effective operational efficiency when managing the Operating Expenditure to the Total Assets Ratio (OER).

b. Enjoying the competitive advantage due to operational efficiency.

c. Availability of qualified and competent finance and accounting professionals in case of both category pharmaceutical companies.

But in some cases like, in case of A Category Company, Return on Assets (ROA) and Return on Equity (ROE); B Category Company, Return on Assets (ROA), it has been observed that there is an insignificant impact of Operating Expenditure to the Total Assets Ratio (OER$_{it}$) on the financial performance of A and B category pharmaceutical companies and the causes of insignificant result may be due to the following reasons.

a. Sudden change in government norms/regulations/policies.

b. Resignation of fiancé/accounting professionals.

c. Incurring additional expenditure owing to price increase.

d. Over allocation of operating expenditure for the maintenance of total assets.

e. Absence of controlling mechanism.

7.14   Company Category-Wise Ranking as Per Empirical Test Results

As per the empirical test result, Company Category-wise ranking is done in the following.

From Table 7.33, we can visualize the rank of Category A and B pharmaceutical companies on the basis of the significant test results to measure

Table 7.33   Ranking of company category based on empirical test results

Company Type	Total Result (5C x 8R)	Significant Test Result	Insignificant Test Result	Significant Test Result (%)	Insignificant Test Result (%)	Rank as per Significant Test Result (%)
A	40	36	(40-36) = 4	90%	10%	II
B	40	37	(40-37) = 3	92.50%	7.5%	I

C=Columns (5 Nos.), R=Rows (8 Nos.)
Expressed in Table 7.32 as Per Independent Variable Columns 5 Nos. and Rows 8 Nos.
Source Author's own

the impact of research and development (R&D) activities of listed Indian pharmaceutical companies on their financial performance.

As per the significant test result, we can find that B category pharmaceutical companies comprising with Indian origin pharmaceutical companies having turnover more (>) than INR (₹) 300 crores are creating slightly more significant impact of research and development (R&D) activities on financial performance in comparison with A category pharmaceutical companies consisting with subsidiaries of multinational pharmaceutical companies (MNCs) irrespective of any sales turnover operating in the space of Indian Pharmaceutical Industry (IPI). As per the test results, the difference has been observed as only 2.50% (92.50–90%) and derived rank for A category pharmaceutical company is II and B category pharmaceutical company is I.

The best possible relevant reasons for B category pharmaceutical company as Rank-I and A category pharmaceutical company as Rank-II can be any of the following or a combination of the same as stated in the following.

B Category Pharmaceutical Company as Rank-I

a. Aggressive attitude of India's research-centric pharmaceutical companies for conducting research and development (R&D) activities towards innovation and drug discovery which helps to improve the financial performance.

b. Fostering the spirit of innovation and drug discoveries in space of Indian pharmaceutical sector.

A Category Pharmaceutical Company as Rank-II

a. Constant endeavour taken by subsidiary pharmaceutical companies of multinationals (MNCs) on Indian soil through CRAMS (Contract Research and Manufacturing Services) or Joint Venture or Alliances or Partnerships with Indian pharmaceutical companies.

b. Sometimes foreign multinationals (MNCs) take foreign direct investment (FDI) route for performing research and development (R&D) activities.

Reasons for Marginal Difference with respect to B category pharmaceutical companies (Rank-I) comprising with India origin pharmaceutical companies having turnover more than INR ₹ 300 crores.

In the study as per the overall empirical test results, derived marginal difference has been found as 2.5% (92.50–90%) and Rank-I has been obtained in case of B category pharmaceutical companies and it may be due to the following reasons:

a. Enormous support provided by the Government of India (GoI) by introducing new policies or reforming existing policies to encourage the Indian pharmaceutical companies and business enterprises to take the route of innovation and drug discoveries as well as unlocking India's potential for leadership in pharmaceutical innovation.

b. Focusing on infrastructural development with the help of state of the art technological inputs and facilities.

c. Investing adequate amount of financial resources sometime 18% to 20% of company's turnover in the area of pharmaceutical drug discovery and innovation by setting appropriate research and development (R&D) strategy.

d. Improvement of manufacturing facilities in the scientific areas of injectable and tablets.

e. Focusing improvement on Active Pharmaceutical Ingredient (API) capabilities.

f. Allocation of spending used for biologics and developing information technology as well as information technology-enabled services (IT and ITes) and automating process.

g. Performing pharmacokinetic and bioequivalence studies to facilitate the introduction of generic or branded generic drugs into the international market.

h. Setting up state of the art clinical trial facility, deploying research scientists in modern in-house laboratories.

i. Engaging in collaborative research approach by establishing a strong connect between industry and academia.

j. Dedicated and painstaking efforts being rendered by the qualified pool of scientists rendering their services for drug discoveries with purity, patience and perseverance.

k. Immense support and cooperation provided from the financial institutions by providing financial assistance to the Indian pharmaceutical companies for conducting different research and development (R&D) activities in the pharmaceutical sector.

Reasons for Marginal Difference with respect to a category pharmaceutical companies (Rank-II) subsidiaries of multinational (MNC) pharmaceutical companies operating in India.

The slight difference (2.5%) which has been found in the study between the Indian pharmaceutical companies and subsidiaries of multinational (MNC) pharmaceutical companies may be due to the following reasons.

a. All multinational pharmaceutical companies having operation worldwide and hence there may be certain less concentration in Indian perspectives.

b. As far as the regulatory compliance and legitimate protocols are concerned with regard to research and development (R&D) activities and clinical trial, it might so happen foreign multinationals are obtaining more benefit in other countries in comparison with India.

c. There may be some specific country preference for foreign multinational (MNC) pharmaceutical companies depending on various factors where country India is not a preferred destination for R&D investment in drug and pharmaceutical sector.

7.15   CONCLUSION

In this study, it has been found that the continuous efforts being rendered by Indian pharmaceutical companies in the areas of research and development (R&D) activities by developing their research and development (R&D) infrastructural facilities with the help of state-of-the-art technological inputs, innovation and research breakthrough and drug discoveries are constantly taking place.

After providing intense efforts in a sustained manner and after waiting longer period of time (sometime the waiting time is 15–20 years), when a research breakthrough and innovation is taking place, then that innovative healthcare solution is being served to the needy patient fraternities with the help of right promotional strategy to cater the unmet healthcare needs. As a result, these innovative pharmaceutical companies can witness a satisfactory financial performance and enjoy the financial performance.

In this study, it has been closely observed that the amount which is being incurred by listed Indian pharmaceutical companies in the areas of research and development (R&D) expenditure which has been measured by Research and Development Intensity (RDI) for this study creates positive impact on financial performance which has been measures by Sales Turnover, Return on Assets (ROA), Return on Equity (ROE) and Market Capitalization for this study.

It has been found that research and development (R&D) expenditure of Indian pharmaceutical companies is gaining importance day by day. About 18 to 20% of sales turnover have been incurred on research and development (R&D) activities by the research-centric reputed Indian pharmaceutical companies.

As we know that research and development (R&D) activities of Indian pharmaceutical companies depend on the infrastructural development and hence initiatives have also been taken for R&D Infrastructural Development by Indian pharmaceutical companies and some of the initiatives taken by Indian pharmaceutical companies are: manufacturing facilities for injectable and tablets and also increasing its Active Pharmaceutical Ingredient (API) capabilities, allocation of spending used for biologics and developing information technology and automating process, performing pharmacokinetic and bioequivalence studies to facilitate the introduction of generic or branded generic drugs into the international market, setting up state-of-the-art clinical trial facility, deploying research scientists in modern in-house laboratories.

To establish empirical relationship between research and development activities and financial performance of Indian pharmaceutical companies an empirical analysis with regard to the four hypotheses.

The first hypothesis relates research and development (R&D) expenditure with Sales Turnover. The result shows significant positive relation, i.e., when the Research and Development (RDI) expenditure has increased, Sales Turnover (Ln_ST) has also been increased in all categories of companies. This is happening because pharmaceutical companies are marketing innovative healthcare solution to the end users at large and catering the unmet healthcare needs of the patients.

The second hypothesis relates Research and Development (RDI) expenditures with Return on Assets (ROA). The results of the study show also significant positive relation, i.e. when Research and Development (RDI) expenditure has increased, Return on Assets (ROA) has also increased.

The third hypothesis relates Research and Development expenditures with Return on Equity (ROE). It also ensures a significant increase in the performance of Indian pharmaceutical companies.

The fourth hypothesis relates Research and Development expenditures (RDI) with Market Capitalization (Ln_MC). This study has confirmed significant increase in the R&D expenditures (Research and Development Intensity, i.e. RDI) that enable the pharmaceutical companies to increase the Market Capitalization (Ln_MC) of the companies.

Thus, in this study, it has been found that all category Indian pharmaceutical companies have showed significant impact of Research and Development Intensity (RDI) on the financial performance which is measured by Sales Turnover, Return on Assets (ROA), Return on Equity (ROE) and Market Capitalization (Ln_MC).

The reasons in favour of significant result may be due to attitude or inclination of the pharmaceutical companies making large investment in research and development (R&D) activities. Moreover, an innovative healthcare solution which is the outcome of research and development (R&D) activities always acts as a catalyst for ensuring high financial returns and strategic advantage.

REFERENCES

Nandy, M. (2020). Is there any impact of R&D on financial performance? Evidence from Indian pharmaceutical companies. *FIIB Business Review, 9*(4), 319–334. https://doi.org/10.1177/2319714520981816

Nidumolu, R. (2009). *Why sustainability is now the key driver of innovation?* Retrieved from https://hbr.org/2009/09/why-sustainability-is-now-the-key-driver-of-innovation

Pal, B., & Nandy, M. (2019). Innovation and business sustainability (IBS): Empirical evidence from Indian pharmaceutical industry (IPI). *Artificial Intelligence for Engineering Design, Analysis and Manufacturing, 33*(2), 117–128. https://doi.org/10.1017/S0890060419000040

Tyage, S., & Nauriyal, D. K. (2016). Profitability determinants in Indian drugs and pharmaceutical industry: An analysis of pre and post TRIPS period. *Eurasian Journal of Business and Economics, 9*(17), 1–21. https://www.ejbe.org/EJBE2016Vol09No17p001TYAGI-NAURIYAL.pdf

INDEX

© The Editor(s) (if applicable) and The Author(s), under exclusive license to Springer Nature Singapore Pte Ltd. 2022
M. Nandy, *Relationship between R&D and Financial Performance in Indian Pharmaceutical Industry*,
https://doi.org/10.1007/978-981-16-6921-7

Printed by Printforce, United Kingdom